one-dish salad meals

good carbs salads • high protein salads • superfood salads • classic salads

mc
rae
PUBLISHING

mc rae PUBLISHING

This book was conceived, edited, and designed by McRae Publishing Ltd London

www.mcraepublishing.co.uk

NOTE TO OUR READERS
Eating eggs or egg whites that are not completely cooked poses the possibility of salmonella food poisoning. The risk is greater for pregnant women, the elderly, the very young, and persons with impaired immune systems. If you are concerned about salmonella, you can use reconstituted powdered egg whites or pasteurized eggs.

Culinary Notebooks series

Project Director Anne McRae
Art Director Marco Nardi

ONE-DISH SALAD MEALS
Photography Brent Parker Jones
Text Carla Bardi
Editing Christine Price, Daphne Trotter
Food Styling Lee Blaylock
Food Preparation and Assistant Stylists Mark Hockenhull, Milli Lee
Layouts Aurora Granata

ISBN 978-1-910122-22-8

Printed in China

contents

getting started

Here you will find 100 healthy, light, and delicious recipes for hearty salads that can be served as a meal in themselves. Most of the recipes are simple to prepare. To help you choose the right one, we have rated them for difficulty: 1 (simple), 2 (fairly simple), or 3 (challenging). In these two pages we have highlighted 25 of the most enticing dishes, just to get you started!

 QUICK

POTATO & TUNA SALAD
with pesto

GRILLED CHICKEN
SALAD with olives, mint
& yogurt

CHICKEN & GARBANZO BEAN SALAD

QUINOA SALAD
with zucchini & feta
cheese

TUNA & BEAN
salad

BARLEY, FAVA & GOAT
CHEESE salad

AVOCADO, FAVA & FETA
salad

VEGETARIAN

FARRO TABBOULEH with boiled eggs

COLESLAW

PINZIMONIO

INTERNATIONAL

GADO GADO
Indonesian salad

SPICY NOODLE SALAD
with shrimp

TACO SALAD
with fresh corn

THAI SEAFOOD
salad

PANZANELLA
Tuscan bread salad

POTATO SALAD
with bacon & blue cheese

HONEY & MUSTARD
chicken salad

EDITOR'S CHOICE

CHEESE, WALNUT
& BLUEBERRY salad

GREEK salad

STEAK SALAD with onion rings & candied walnuts

| BEST PASTA SALAD | BEST VEGAN SALAD | BEST MEATY SALAD | BEST SEAFOOD SALAD | BEST CLASSIC SALAD |

WHOLE-WHEAT
FARFALLE with pesto
& mozzarella

BARLEY SALAD
with roasted pumpkin

WARM STICKY PORK
with pineapple salsa

SEAFOOD
salad

COBB salad

good carbs salads

POTATO SALAD
with bacon & blue cheese

1 pound (500 g) new potatoes, halved or quartered, depending on size

Sea salt flakes

6 tablespoons (90 ml) extra-virgin olive oil

2 red onions, each sliced into 6 wedges

4 slices smoked bacon, rinds removed and cut into large pieces

5 ounces (150 g) white mushrooms, sliced

1 tablespoon wholegrain mustard

1 tablespoon red wine vinegar

3 cups (150 g) mixed watercress and spinach salad greens

4 ounces (120 g) blue cheese, such as Roquefort, Gorgonzola, or Danish Blue, crumbled

Serves 4 • Preparation 15 minutes • Cooking 50–60 minutes
Difficulty 1

1. Preheat the oven to 425°F (220°C/gas 7).

2. Put the potatoes in a roasting pan. Season with salt and drizzle with 4 tablespoons of the oil. Roast for 20 minutes.

3. Add the onions to the pan, stirring gently. Roast for 20–25 minutes more, until the potatoes are golden brown and the onions have softened and begun to caramelize. Remove from the oven and let cool slightly.

4. Heat a large frying pan over medium heat. Dry-fry the bacon until crisp and golden, about 5 minutes. Add the mushrooms and simmer until softened, about 5 minutes.

5. Whisk the mustard, vinegar, and remaining 2 tablespoons of oil in a bowl until combined.

6. Put the potatoes, onions, bacon, and mushrooms in a large bowl with the salad greens. Drizzle with the dressing and toss well. Divide among four serving plates, sprinkle with the blue cheese, and serve.

If you liked this recipe, you will love these as well.

RIGATONI SALAD with grilled summer veggies

POTATO SALAD with cherry tomatoes & olives

POTATO & TUNA SALAD with pesto

Carbs have been getting some bad rap recently, but you need to know that there are good carbs and bad carbs. Whole grain carbs like those found in brown or wild rice and whole-wheat pasta, are richer in dietary fiber and important nutrients than refined white rice or pasta. They also taste better and will make you feel fuller for longer, thereby helping to avoid weight gain due to overeating.

WHOLE-WHEAT FARFALLE
with pesto & mozzarella

Pesto
2	cups (100 g) fresh basil leaves
2	cloves garlic, coarsely chopped
1/2	teaspoon sea salt flakes
1/2	cup (60 g) pine nuts, lightly toasted
1/3	cup (40 g) freshly grated Parmesan cheese
1/2	cup (120 ml) extra-virgin olive oil

Salad
1	pound (500 g) whole-wheat (wholemeal) farfalle (bow ties)
2	tablespoons balsamic vinegar
1/2	cup fresh basil leaves
24	cherry tomatoes, halved
8	ounces (250 g) baby bocconcini (mozzarella cheese balls), halved
	Freshly ground sea salt and black pepper

Serves 4–6 • Preparation 15 minutes • Cooking 10–12 minutes
Difficulty 1

Pesto
1. Combine the basil, garlic, and salt in a food processor and blend for 5 seconds. Add the pine nuts, cheese, and half the oil and blend for 5 more seconds. Scrape down the sides, add the remaining oil, and blend until smooth.

Salad
1. Cook the pasta in a large pot of salted boiling until al dente. Drain well and transfer to a large bowl. Shake well to cool a little and set aside.

2. Combine the pesto and balsamic vinegar in a small bowl. Pour over the pasta in the bowl and toss to combine.

3. Add the basil, cherry tomatoes, and bocconcini. Season with salt and pepper. Toss gently, and serve.

If you liked this recipe, you will love these as well.

PASTA SALAD
with shrimp & pesto

RIGATONI SALAD with
grilled summer veggies

PASTA SALAD
with mozza

PASTA SALAD with shrimp & pesto

Pesto

2	cups (100 g) fresh basil leaves
4	tablespoons freshly grated Parmesan cheese
2	tablespoons pine nuts
1/3	cup (90 ml) extra-virgin olive oil
	Freshly ground sea salt and black pepper

Salad

1	pound (500 g) whole-wheat (wholemeal) rigatoni
2	tablespoons extra-virgin olive oil
12	ounces (350 g) peeled cooked shrimp (prawns)
3	tablespoons mayonnaise
	Freshly squeezed juice of 1/2 lemon
3	tablespoons finely chopped fresh parsley
	Whole basil leaves, to garnish
	Lemon wedges, to serve

Serves 4–6 • Preparation 15 minutes • Cooking 10–12 minutes • Difficulty 1

Pesto

1. Combine the basil, Parmesan, and pine nuts in a food processor and chop until smooth. Gradually add the oil. Season with salt and pepper. Set aside.

Salad

1. Cook the pasta in a large pot of salted boiling water until al dente. Drain well and let cool a little in the colander for 2–3 minutes. Combine in a serving bowl with the oil. Toss gently. Add the shrimp and toss again.

2. Whisk the pesto, mayonnaise, and lemon juice in a small bowl. Drizzle the pesto dressing over the pasta and shrimp and toss gently.

3. Add the parsley and toss again. Garnish with the whole basil leaves. Serve with the lemon wedges.

RIGATONI SALAD with grilled summer veggies

1   pound (500 g) whole-wheat (wholemeal) rigatoni

6   tablespoons (90 ml) extra-virgin olive oil

2   red bell peppers (capsicums), seeded, cored, and quartered

2   eggplant (aubergines), with skins, thinly sliced

2   medium zucchini (courgettes), thinly sliced lengthwise

2   tablespoons coarsely chopped fresh basil

2   tablespoons coarsely chopped fresh mint

1   clove garlic, finely chopped

     Freshly ground sea salt and black pepper

Serves 4–6 • Preparation 30 minutes + 1–2 hours to stand • Cooking 20–30 minutes • Difficulty 2

1. Cook the pasta in a large pot of salted boiling water until al dente. Drain well and let cool a little in the colander for 2–3 minutes. Drain well and toss with 2 tablespoons of oil. Set aside while you prepare the vegetables.

2. Preheat the overhead broiler (grill) in the oven and broil the bell peppers, turning them often, until the skins are blackened. Wrap in a brown paper bag or aluminum foil for 10 minutes. Take out of the bag or foil and peel off the skins and all the charred bits.

3. Put the eggplant and zucchini in a grill pan (griddle) and grill until tender and marked with brown lines, 5–10 minutes each batch. Chop all the vegetables coarsely.

4. Toss the pasta with the vegetables in a large salad bowl. Add the basil, mint, and garlic. Season with salt and pepper and drizzle with the remaining 4 tablespoons of oil.

5. Mix well and let stand for 1–2 hours at room temperature before serving.

PASTA SALAD with mozza

Serves 4–6 • Preparation 15 minutes • Cooking 10–12 minutes • Difficulty 2

1	pound (500 g) whole-wheat (wholemeal) farfalle pasta	2	scallions (spring onions), finely chopped
6	tablespoons extra-virgin olive oil	1	celery heart, thinly sliced
14	ounces (400 g) bocconcini (baby mozzarella balls)		Freshly squeezed juice of 1 lemon
16	cherry tomatoes, halved		Freshly ground sea salt and black pepper
		½	teaspoon dried oregano

1. Cook the pasta in a large pot of salted boiling water until al dente. Drain well and let cool in the colander for 2–3 minutes. Toss gently in a serving bowl with 2 tablespoons of oil and set aside.

2. Add the mozzarella, tomatoes, scallions, and celery to the bowl.

3. Whisk the remaining oil, lemon juice, salt, and plenty of pepper in a small bowl. Pour over the salad and toss well. Sprinkle with the oregano, toss again, and serve.

PASTA SALAD with tuna

Serves 4–6 • Preparation 15 minutes • Cooking 10–12 minutes • Difficulty 1

1	pound (500 g) whole-wheat (wholemeal) penne pasta		onions), coarsely chopped
6	tablespoons (90 ml) extra-virgin olive oil	2	stalks celery, sliced
5	ounces (150 g) canned tuna, packed in oil, drained	1	carrot, chopped
		1	clove garlic, minced
20	cherry tomatoes, halved		Freshly ground sea salt and white pepper
1	cup (50 g) mixed black and green olives	2	teaspoons dried oregano
2	scallions (spring	1	tablespoon finely chopped fresh parsley
			Fresh basil, to garnish

1. Cook the pasta in a large pot of salted boiling water until al dente. Drain well and let cool in the colander for 2–3 minutes. Toss gently in a serving bowl with 2 tablespoons of oil and set aside.

2. Crumble the tuna with a fork and add to the bowl. Add the tomatoes, olives, scallions, celery, carrot, and garlic. Drizzle with the remaining 4 tablespoons of oil and season with salt, pepper, and oregano.

3. Add the parsley and basil, toss well, and serve.

PASTA SALAD with grapefruit

Serves 4 • Preparation 25 minutes + 1 hour to chill Cooking 8–10 minutes • Difficulty 1

2	large pink grapefruit		Freshly ground sea salt and white pepper
2	cups (400 g) canned corn (sweetcorn), drained	12	ounces (350 g) whole-wheat (wholemeal) ditalini pasta
2	tablespoons extra-virgin olive oil	1	bunch fresh basil, torn
2	tablespoons mayonnaise		Fresh mint, to garnish

1. Cut the grapefruit in half and remove the flesh. Chop coarsely. Wrap the empty skins in plastic wrap (cling film) and refrigerate until ready to use.

2. Mix the corn, grapefruit flesh, oil, and mayonnaise in a large bowl. Season with salt and white pepper.

3. Cook the pasta in a large pot of salted boiling water until al dente. Drain well and let cool in the colander for 2–3 minutes.

4. Put the pasta in the bowl with the grapefruit mixture and toss gently. Add the basil. Chill for 1 hour.

5. Remove the grapefruit skins from the refrigerator and fill with the pasta mixture. Garnish with the mint, and serve.

PASTA SALAD with eggplant

Serves 4–6 • Preparation 30 minutes + 1 hour to drain Cooking 30–40 minutes • Difficulty 2

1	large eggplant (aubergine), with skin, thickly sliced	1	pound (500 g) whole-wheat (wholemeal) ditalini pasta
	Coarse sea salt	2	tablespoons salt-cured capers, rinsed
8	tablespoons (120 ml) extra-virgin olive oil	1	(8-ounce/250-g) jar yellow bell peppers (capsicums), drained
1	onion, finely chopped	1	cup (100 g) olives
2	cloves garlic, minced		Fresh basil, to garnish
	Sea salt flakes		

1. Put the eggplant in a colander and sprinkle with the coarse salt. Let drain for 1 hour. Cut into small cubes.

2. Heat 5 tablespoons of oil in a large frying pan over medium-high heat. Fry the eggplant until tender and golden, 5–7 minutes. Drain on paper towels.

3. Heat the remaining 3 tablespoons of oil in a small saucepan over medium heat. Add the onion, garlic, and salt and sauté until golden, about 5 minutes. Cover and simmer over low heat for 15 minutes.

4. Cook the pasta in salted boiling water until al dente. Drain and let cool in the colander for 2–3 minutes. Transfer to a bowl and toss with the eggplant, capers, bell peppers, onions, olives, basil, and serve.

You could also use canned pineapple chunks. Make sure they are well drained before adding them to the noodles.

SPICY NOODLE SALAD with shrimp

Dressing

1	fresh red chili, seeded and sliced
1	clove garlic
1	teaspoon brown sugar
	Freshly squeezed juice of 2 limes
1½	teaspoons Thai fish sauce

Salad

12	ounces (350 g) rice or soba noodles
1	small sweet fresh pineapple
3	cups (150 g) bean sprouts
8	ounces (250 g) cooked shrimp (prawns), peeled and deveined
1	small cucumber, peeled, seeded, and sliced
20	cherry tomatoes, halved
½	cup fresh mint leaves
½	cup (60 g) toasted, salted cashews

Serves 4-6 • Preparation 20 minutes • Cooking 5–10 minutes
Difficulty 1

Dressing

1. Pound the chili, garlic, and sugar to a paste with a pestle and mortar. Stir in the lime juice and fish sauce. Set aside until ready to use.

Salad

1. Cook the noodles following the instructions on the package. Drain well and transfer to a large salad bowl.

2. Peel, quarter, and core the pineapple, then slice into bite-size pieces. Add to the bowl with the noodles, including any juices from the slicing.

3. Add the bean sprouts, shrimp, cucumber, and tomatoes to the bowl. Toss gently. Top with the mint and cashews.

4. Drizzle with the dressing, and serve.

If you liked this recipe, you will love these as well.

PASTA SALAD
with shrimp & pesto

SOBA NOODLE SALAD
with dipping sauce

**SOBA NOODLE
& SHRIMP SALAD**
with papaya

SOBA NOODLE SALAD with dipping sauce

Dipping Sauce
1½	cups (375 ml) dashi stock
¼	cup (60 ml) rice wine
¼	cup (60 ml) soy sauce
1	teaspoon sesame oil
1	clove garlic, finely chopped
1	teaspoon finely grated fresh ginger

Noodles
12	ounces (350 g) dried soba (buckwheat) noodles
1	medium carrot, cut into thin matchsticks
1	red bell pepper (capsicum), seeded and thinly sliced
1	nori sheet, thinly sliced
1	teaspoon white sesame seeds
1	teaspoon black sesame seeds
3	scallions (spring onions), thinly sliced
¼	cup (20 g) pickled ginger

Serves 4 • Preparation 20 minutes • Cooking 10 minutes • Difficulty 1

Dipping Sauce

1. Combine all the ingredients in a small saucepan over medium heat and bring to a boil. Remove from the heat and set aside to cool.

Noodles

1. Cook the noodles following the instructions on the package. Drain well.

2. Combine the noodles, carrot, and bell pepper in a large bowl and toss to combine.

3. Place the nori and sesame seeds in a small frying pan and toast over medium-low heat until the sesame seeds are golden and the nori is crisp, about 1 minute.

4. Divide the noodles evenly among four serving bowls and sprinkle with the nori and sesame seed mixture. Top with the scallions and pickled ginger. Serve cold or chilled with the dipping sauce.

SOBA NOODLE & SHRIMP SALAD with papaya

12 ounces (350 g) soba noodles

1/3 cup (90 ml) tamarind concentrate

2 tablespoons light brown sugar

4 tablespoons (60 ml) sesame oil

1 tablespoon freshly squeezed lime juice

1/2 teaspoon cayenne pepper

1 cup fresh cilantro (coriander) leaves + extra, to garnish

1 small red onion, thinly sliced

1 papaya (about 1 pound/ 500 g), peeled, seeds removed, and thinly sliced

1/2 cup (60 g) salted peanuts

Freshly ground sea salt and black pepper

3 cloves garlic, thinly sliced

1 pound (500 g) large shrimp (prawns), peeled and deveined

1/2 teaspoon ground coriander

Serves 4 • Preparation 20 minutes • Cooking 10–15 minutes
Difficulty 2

1. Cook the noodles following the instructions on the package. Drain well.

2. Whisk the tamarind concentrate, sugar, 2 tablespoons of oil, lime juice, and cayenne in a bowl. Add the noodles, cilantro, onion, half the papaya, and peanuts. Season with salt and pepper and toss to combine.

3. Heat the remaining 2 tablespoons of oil over low heat in a large frying pan. Add the garlic and sauté until golden brown, about 5 minutes. Remove the garlic and set aside on a paper towel.

4. Increase the heat to medium-high, add the shrimp, coriander, salt, and pepper, and sauté until the shrimp are cooked through, about 3 minutes.

5. Divide the noodles and shrimp evenly among four large bowls. Top each serving with the remaining papaya, garlic, and cilantro, and serve.

Make this salad in the spring when fava beans (broad beans) are fresh and succulent.

BARLEY, FAVA & GOAT CHEESE salad

Dressing

¹/₃   cup (90 ml) extra-virgin olive oil

¹/₄   cup (60 ml) freshly squeezed lemon juice

      Freshly ground sea salt and black pepper

Salad

4   cups (1 liter) vegetable stock

1   pound (500 g) fresh or frozen fava (broad) beans

1¹/₂   cups (300 g) pearl barley

1   cup finely chopped fresh parsley

20   cherry tomatoes, halved

1   cup (120 g) hazelnuts, toasted

7   ounces (200 g) goat cheese, crumbled or cut into small chunks

Serves 4 • Preparation 15 minutes + 15 minutes to cool • Cooking 45 minutes • Difficulty 1

Dressing

1. Whisk the oil, lemon juice, salt, and pepper in a small bowl. Cover and chill until ready to serve.

Salad

1. Bring the stock to a boil in a medium saucepan. Add the fava beans and cook until they float, 3–4 minutes. Using a slotted spoon, transfer to a bowl and run under cold water.

2. Add the pearl barley to the stock and simmer over low heat until tender, about 40 minutes, or according to the time on the package. Drain the barley, then set aside to cool for 15 minutes.

3. Mix the parsley into the barley. Drizzle with the dressing and mix again. Divide evenly among four serving bowls, Sprinkle with the cherry tomatoes, hazelnuts, and goat cheese, and serve.

If you liked this recipe, you will love these as well.

QUINOA SALAD
with feta & almonds

SPELT, CORN & FETA
salad

BARLEY SALAD
with roasted pumpkin

QUINOA SALAD with corn & beans

Spicy Vinaigrette

1/3	cup (90 ml) extra-virgin olive oil
2	tablespoons freshly squeezed lemon juice
2	tablespoons raspberry vinegar
1	tablespoon sherry
1	teaspoon finely grated lemon zest
1/2	teaspoon brown sugar
2	teaspoons horseradish cream
	Dash of Tabasco sauce

Salad

1 1/2	cups (300 g) quinoa
3	cups (750 ml) water
2	red bell peppers (capsicums), diced
1	(14-ounce/400-g) can pinto beans, drained and rinsed
1	cup (200 g) canned corn (sweetcorn)
6	radishes, thinly sliced
1	scallion (spring onion), chopped

Serves 4 • Preparation 15 minutes + 30 minutes to cool • Cooking 15 minutes • Difficulty 1

Spicy Vinaigrette

1. Whisk the oil, lemon juice, vinegar, sherry, lemon zest, brown sugar, horseradish cream, and Tabasco sauce in a small bowl. Set aside until ready to use.

Salad

1. Rinse the quinoa thoroughly under cold running water.

2. Pour the water into a medium saucepan and bring to a boil. Stir in the quinoa, reduce the heat, and cover. Simmer until the water is absorbed and the quinoa is cooked, about 15 minutes. Drain well and set aside to cool, about 30 minutes.

3. Combine the quinoa, bell peppers, beans, corn, radishes, and scallion in a salad bowl. Drizzle with the vinaigrette, toss gently, and serve.

QUINOA SALAD with grapefruit

Salad

$1^1/_2$ cups (300 g) quinoa

3 cups (750 ml) apple juice

1 small red bell pepper (capsicum), diced

4 tablespoons finely chopped fresh parsley

3 tablespoons finely chopped fresh mint

2 pink grapefruit, peeled, halved, and broken into segments

1 small onion, sliced

Warm Citrus Dressing

Freshly squeezed juice of 1 grapefruit

2 tablespoons extra-virgin olive oil or hazelnut oil

1 teaspoon honey

Serves 4–6 • Preparation 20 minutes + 30 minutes to cool • Cooking 15 minutes • Difficulty 1

Salad

1. Rinse the quinoa thoroughly under cold running water.

2. Bring the apple juice to a boil in a medium saucepan over medium heat. Stir in the quinoa. Cover and simmer over low heat until the apple juice is absorbed and the quinoa is cooked, about 15 minutes. Drain well and set aside to cool, about 30 minutes.

3. Transfer the cooled quinoa to a salad bowl and add the bell pepper, parsley, mint, grapefruit, and onion. Toss well.

Warm Citrus Dressing

1. Combine the grapefruit juice, oil, and honey in a small saucepan over low heat. Simmer until the honey is dissolved.

2. Drizzle the dressing over the salad, toss gently, and serve.

Quinoa, pronounced keen-wa, looks like a grain but is actually a member of the grass family. It is gluten-free, making it an ideal food choice for people with gluten intolerance. It is rich in protein, calcium, and iron, and an excellent source of magnesium.

QUINOA SALAD with feta & almonds

Salad
2	tablespoons extra-virgin olive oil
1	teaspoon ground coriander
$1/2$	teaspoon turmeric
$1^1/_2$	cups (300 g) quinoa, rinsed
$2^1/_2$	cups (620 ml) boiling water
$1/2$	cup (60 g) toasted flaked almonds + extra, to garnish
5	ounces (150 g) feta cheese, crumbled
$1/2$	cup coarsely chopped fresh parsley + extra, to garnish

Dressing
$1/4$	cup (60 ml) extra-virgin olive oil
	Freshly squeezed juice of $1/2$ lemon
	Freshly ground sea salt and black pepper

Serves 4 • Preparation 15 minutes + 30 minutes to cool • Cooking 15–20 minutes • Difficulty 1

Salad

1. Heat 1 tablespoon of oil in a large frying pan. Add the coriander and turmeric and sauté until fragrant, about 1 minute.

2. Add the quinoa and sauté until you can hear gentle popping sounds, about 1 minute. Stir in the boiling water and simmer over very low heat until the water has been absorbed and the quinoa grains are tender, about 15 minutes.

3. Set aside to cool, about 30 minutes. Stir in the almonds, feta, and parsley.

Dressing

1. Whisk the oil, lemon juice, salt, and pepper in a small bowl.

2. Drizzle the dressing over the salad, toss gently, and serve, garnished with extra parsley and almonds.

If you liked this recipe, you will love these as well.

QUINOA SALAD
with corn & beans

QUINOA SALAD
with grapefruit

BULGUR SALAD
with zucchini flowers

BULGUR SALAD with zucchini flowers

2	cups (300 g) fine or medium bulgur
3	zucchini (courgettes), cut into thin batons
1	tablespoon freshly squeezed lemon juice
$\frac{1}{2}$	cup (120 ml) pesto (see page 8)
$\frac{1}{4}$	cup (50 g) pine nuts, toasted
$\frac{1}{3}$	cup (90 ml) extra-virgin olive oil
	Freshly ground sea salt and black pepper
4	cups (200 g) arugula (rocket)
$\frac{1}{2}$	teaspoon sweet paprika
6	very fresh zucchini (courgette) flowers, coarsely chopped

Serves 4-6 • Preparation 15 minutes + 1 hour to soak • Difficulty 1

1. Put the bulgur in a medium bowl and add plenty of cold water to cover. Set aside for 1 hour.

2. Drain the bulgur in a colander lined with a clean kitchen cloth. Scoop the bulgur up in the cloth and squeeze out all the excess moisture.

3. Transfer the bulgur to a salad bowl. Add the zucchini, lemon juice, pesto, pine nuts, and 3 tablespoons of the oil. Season with salt and pepper and toss well.

4. Arrange the arugula in four to six serving dishes.

5. Spoon the salad on top of the arugula. Dust with the paprika and top with the zucchini flowers. Drizzle with the remaining oil, and serve.

SPELT, CORN & FETA salad

Salad

1	pound (500 g) spelt (or pearl barley)
1	large red bell pepper (capsicum)
8	ounces (250 g) fresh mozzarella cheese, drained and cut into small cubes
1	cup (120 g) canned corn (sweetcorn), drained
1	tablespoon finely chopped fresh parsley
1	tablespoon finely chopped fresh basil
1/2	tablespoon finely chopped fresh marjoram
1	clove garlic, finely chopped

Dressing

1/3	cup (90 ml) extra-virgin olive oil
	Freshly squeezed juice of 1 lemon
	Freshly ground sea salt and black pepper

Serves 6–8 • Preparation 30 minutes + 15 minutes to cool • Cooking 35–40 minutes • Difficulty 2

Salad

1. Cook the spelt in a large pot of salted boiling water until tender, 35–40 minutes. Drain well and set aside to cool for 15 minutes. Place in a large salad bowl.

2. While the spelt is cooking, preheat an overhead broiler (grill) to high. Broil the bell pepper, turning often, until charred all over, 15–20 minutes. Wrap the bell pepper in aluminum foil and let rest for 10 minutes. Unwrap and remove the skin and seeds. Slice thinly.

3. Add the bell pepper, mozzarella, corn, parsley, basil, marjoram, and garlic to the bowl with the spelt. Toss well.

Dressing

1. Whisk the oil and lemon juice in a small bowl with a fork. Season with salt and pepper.

2. Drizzle the dressing over the salad. Toss well, and serve.

This hearty salad is great in the wintertime when pumpkins and squash are in season.

BARLEY SALAD with roasted pumpkin

Dressing
$1/3$	cup (90 ml) extra-virgin olive oil
$1/4$	cup (60 ml) balsamic vinegar
1	tablespoon Dijon mustard
1	clove garlic, minced
	Freshly ground sea salt and black pepper

Salad
1	small pumpkin or butternut squash, peeled and cut into bite-size pieces
2	tablespoons extra-virgin olive oil
	Sea salt flakes
$1^1/2$	cups (300 g) pearl barley
12	ounces (350 g) flowering broccoli, cut into medium-size florets
1	cup (75 g) sun-dried tomatoes, in oil, drained and coarsely chopped
1	small red onion, diced
3	tablespoons pumpkin seeds
1	tablespoon salt-cured capers, rinsed
20	black olives, pitted
1	cup coarsely chopped fresh basil

Serves 4–6 • Preparation 15 minutes • Cooking 40–50 minutes Difficulty 2

Dressing
1. Whisk the oil, vinegar, mustard, and garlic in a small bowl. Season with salt and pepper and whisk again. Set aside.

Salad
1. Preheat the oven to 400°F (200°C/gas 6). Place the pumpkin on a rimmed baking sheet and toss with the oil. Season with salt and roast for 20 minutes.

2. Boil the barley until tender, about 40 minutes, or for the time indicated on the package.

3. Drain the barley, then transfer to a bowl and drizzle with the dressing. Mix well and let cool.

4. Boil the broccoli in salted water until just tender, then drain and let sit in the colander for a few minutes to cool. Add the broccoli and remaining ingredients to the barley. Toss well, and serve.

If you liked this recipe, you will love these as well.

BARLEY, FAVA & GOAT CHEESE salad

QUINOA SALAD with feta & almonds

SPELT, CORN & FETA salad

TACO SALAD with fresh corn

3	ears (cobs) corn, husks and silk removed
3	corn tortillas, cut into 16 wedges each
3/4	cup (180 ml) plain yogurt
	Freshly squeezed juice of 2 limes
1/2	cup fresh cilantro (coriander) leaves
1	small jalapeño chili, seeded and finely chopped
1/2	teaspoon coarse sea salt
1	pound (500 g) ground (minced) turkey
1	teaspoon chili powder
1	teaspoon ground cumin
3	cups (150 g) iceberg lettuce, torn
1	cup (200 g) canned black beans, drained
12	cherry tomatoes, halved
1/2	red onion, sliced
1	small mango, peeled, seeded, and cut into 1/4-inch (5-mm) thick wedges

Serves 4 • Preparation 30 minutes • Cooking 20–30 minutes
Difficulty 1

1. Bring a large pot of water to a boil over high heat. Add the corn and simmer until tender, 5–10 minutes. Transfer to a plate and let cool. Slice the kernels off the ears. Place in a small bowl, and set aside (you should have about 2 cups).

2. Preheat the oven to 350°F (180°C/gas 4). Spread the tortilla wedges in a single layer on a baking sheet. Bake until crisp, turning once, about 10 minutes. Set aside to cool.

3. Whisk the yogurt, juice from 1 lime, cilantro, jalapeño, and salt in a medium bowl. Set aside.

4. Sauté the turkey in a large frying pan over medium heat until lightly browned, 8–10 minutes. Stir in the chili powder, cumin, and remaining lime juice.

5. Transfer the turkey mixture to a large serving bowl. Add the lettuce, beans, tomatoes, onion, mango, and reserved corn and tortillas. Toss well to combine. Drizzle with the yogurt dressing, and serve.

POTATO SALAD with cherry tomatoes & olives

2 pounds (1 kg) new potatoes
1 cup (100 g) green olives, pitted
1 cup (100 g) black olives, pitted
2 tablespoons finely chopped fresh basil
1 clove garlic, finely chopped
1 tablespoon white wine vinegar
1 celery heart, thinly sliced
16 cherry tomatoes, halved
1/3 cup (90 ml) extra-virgin olive oil
Sea salt flakes

Serves 6 • Preparation 15 minutes + 1 hour to cool • Cooking 15–20 minutes • Difficulty 1

1. Cook the potatoes in a large pot of salted boiling water until tender, 15–20 minutes. Drain well and let cool slightly.

2. Place both types of olive in a large salad bowl. Add the basil, garlic, and vinegar, and mix well.

3. Cut the potatoes in half and add to the salad bowl. Toss gently and let cool completely, about 1 hour.

4. Add the celery and cherry tomatoes. Drizzle with oil and season with salt. Toss again, and serve.

The humble potato is a powerhouse of nutrients and energy. Potatoes are a very good source of vitamin B6 and a good source of potassium, copper, vitamin C, manganese, phosphorus, niacin, dietary fiber, and pantothenic acid. They also contain compounds called kukoamines which are believed to help lower blood pressure.

POTATO & TUNA SALAD with pesto

1½	pounds (750 g) new potatoes, halved if large
1	recipe pesto (see page 8)
8	ounces (250 g) green beans, trimmed and halved
2	cups (100 g) baby spinach leaves
	Freshly ground sea salt and black pepper
12	cherry tomatoes, halved
1	(6-ounce/180-g) can tuna, drained and flaked

Serves 4 • Preparation 15 minutes • Cooking 8–10 minutes • Difficulty 1

1. Put the potatoes in a pan of lightly salted boiling water, bring to a boil, then simmer until tender, 8–10 minutes, depending on their size.

2. Prepare the pesto. Our recipe will make about twice as much as you will need for this salad. Place the rest in a jar, cover; it will keep in the refrigerator for 2–3 days.

3. Add the green beans to the potatoes for the last 3 minutes of cooking time.

4. Drain the potatoes and beans, shaking thoroughly in the colander to dry and cool a little. Transfer to a salad bowl.

5. Stir in the spinach leaves so that they wilt a little from the warmth of the vegetables. Season with salt and pepper. Sprinkle the tomatoes and tuna on top.

6. Drizzle with the pesto, toss gently, and serve.

If you liked this recipe, you will love these as well.

POTATO SALAD with bacon & blue cheese

TACO SALAD with fresh corn

POTATO SALAD with cherry tomatoes & olives

BAKED RICE salad

1 small onion
3 cloves
6 tablespoons (90 ml) extra-virgin olive oil
1 1/2 cups (300 g) short-grain rice
1 bay leaf
2 1/2 cups (620 ml) vegetable stock, boiling
5 ounces (150 g) fresh or frozen green beans, chopped
1 cup (150 g) fresh or frozen peas
1 large red bell pepper (capsicum)
6 pickled gherkins, drained and chopped
1 tablespoon salt-cured capers, rinsed
3 tablespoons white wine vinegar
  Sea salt flakes
1 cup (120 g) canned corn (sweetcorn)
3 cups (150 g) arugula (rocket), chopped

Serves 4 • Preparation 30 minutes • Cooking 40–50 minutes • Difficulty 2

1. Preheat the oven to 350°F (180°C/gas 4). Stud the onion with the cloves.

2. Heat 2 tablespoons of oil in a large Dutch oven or casserole over medium heat. Add the onion and sauté for 2–3 minutes. Add the rice and mix well. Add the bay leaf and stock. Cover and bake until the rice has absorbed all the water and is al dente, about 20 minutes. Set aside to cool.

3. Cook the green beans in a pot of salted boiling water until just tender, 5–7 minutes. Drain well and let cool. Cook the peas in a small pot of salted boiling water until just tender, 3–5 minutes. Drain well and let cool.

4. Preheat an overhead broiler (grill) to high. Broil the pepper until charred, 15–20 minutes. Wrap in aluminum foil and let rest for 10 minutes. Remove the skin and seeds. Slice thinly.

5. Chop the gherkins, capers, remaining 4 tablespoons of oil, and vinegar in a food processor until smooth. Transfer the rice to a salad bowl. Remove and discard the onion, cloves, and bay leaf. Add the beans, peas, corn, pepper, and arugula.

6. Drizzle with the dressing and toss gently. Serve lukewarm.

MEDITERRANEAN RICE salad

1   large yellow bell pepper
     (capsicum)
1   large red bell pepper
     (capsicum)
2   cups (400 g) short-grain rice
1   small bunch fresh basil, torn
6   tablespoons (90 ml) extra-
     virgin olive oil
2   tablespoons butter
2   cloves garlic, finely chopped
8   anchovy fillets
1   tablespoon finely chopped
     fresh mint
1   tablespoon brine-cured
     capers, drained

Serves 4–6 • Preparation 30 minutes + 30 minutes to cool • Cooking 15 minutes • Difficulty 2

1. Preheat an overhead broiler (grill) to high. Broil the bell peppers until charred, 15–20 minutes. Wrap in aluminum foil and let rest for 10 minutes. Remove the skin and seeds. Chop coarsely and place in a large bowl.

2. Cook the rice in a large pot of lightly salted water until tender, about 15 minutes.

3. Drain well and leave in the colander to cool for 5–10 minutes. Mix the rice in a bowl with the bell peppers, half the basil, and 4 tablespoons (60 ml) of oil.

4. Melt the butter in a small frying pan over medium heat. Add the garlic and sauté until pale gold, 3–4 minutes. Add the remaining 2 tablespoons of oil and the anchovies. Stir until the anchovies are dissolved.

5 Spoon the anchovy sauce over the rice. Sprinkle with the remaining basil, the mint, and capers, toss gently, and serve.

EASY RICE salad

Serves 4-6 • Preparation 15 minutes • Cooking 15-40 minutes • Difficulty 1

2	cups (400 g) white or brown rice	2	tablespoons brine-cured capers, drained
1	cup (150 g) frozen peas	12	black olives, pitted and coarsely chopped
24	cherry tomatoes, halved	1	sweet red onion, finely chopped or sliced
5	ounces (150 g) Fontina or Emmental cheese, cut into small cubes	8	basil leaves, torn
1	cucumber, peeled and cut into small cubes	1/4	cup (60 ml) extra-virgin olive oil
			Sea salt flakes

1. Cook the rice in a large pot of salted, boiling water until tender, about 15 minutes for white rice or 30-40 minutes for brown.

2. Drain well and leave in the colander to cool for 5-10 minutes. Transfer the rice to a large bowl.

3. Cook the peas in a small pot of salted boiling water until tender, about 5 minutes. Drain well and cool under cold running water. Drain again and place in the salad bowl.

4. Add the cherry tomatoes, cheese, cucumber, capers, olives, onion, and basil to the bowl with the rice.

WARM RED RICE salad

Serves 4-6 • Preparation 15 minutes • Cooking 30-40 minutes • Difficulty 1

1½	cups (300 g) Camargue red rice or other short-grain colored or brown rice	1	unwaxed lemon
8	sun-dried tomatoes in extra-virgin olive oil, drained and chopped, reserving 2 tablespoons of the oil	1	tablespoon brine-cured capers, drained
		1/2	cup finely chopped fresh parsley
			Freshly ground sea salt and black pepper
4	tablespoons pine nuts	5	ounces (150 g) Roquefort cheese, crumbled
	Finely grated zest of		

1. Cook the rice in a large pot of salted, boiling water until tender, 30-40 minutes.

2. Drain well and leave in the colander to cool for 5-10 minutes. Transfer the rice to a large bowl.

3. Heat a large frying pan over medium heat. Add the reserved tomato oil, sun-dried tomatoes, pine nuts, lemon zest, and capers and sauté until just beginning to turn golden, 3-4 minutes.

4. Add the rice and sauté until heated through and well mixed, about 2 minutes. Remove from the heat and place in a salad bowl. Top with the parsley and cheese. Toss gently and serve warm.

RICE SALAD with garbanzos

Serves 4-6 • Preparation 15 minutes + 15 minutes to cool Cooking 30-40 minutes • Difficulty 1

2	cups (400 g) brown rice	1	tomatoes, thinly sliced (14-ounce/400-g) can garbanzo beans (chickpeas), drained and rinsed
1/4	cup (60 ml) extra-virgin olive oil		
2	tablespoons red wine vinegar	1	bunch fresh mint, torn + extra, to garnish
1/2	teaspoon red pepper flakes		Freshly ground sea salt and black pepper
1	pound (500 g) cherry		

1. Cook the rice in a large pot of salted, boiling water until tender, 30-40 minutes.

2. Drain well and leave in the colander to cool for 5-10 minutes. Transfer the rice to a large bowl.

3. Whisk the oil, vinegar, and red pepper flakes in a small bowl.

4. Pour the dressing over the rice and toss well. Mix the tomatoes and garbanzo beans into the rice. Add the mint and mix well.

5. Season with salt and pepper. Garnish with the extra mint, and serve.

RICE with tuna & pickles

Serves 6 • Preparation 15 minutes • Cooking 30-40 minutes Difficulty 1

1½	cups (300 g) brown rice		tuna, drained and crumbled
1/3	cup (90 ml) extra-virgin olive oil	2	tablespoons salt-cured capers, rinsed
2	tablespoons freshly squeezed lemon juice	12	stuffed green olives, sliced
1	hard-boiled egg yolk		Freshly ground sea salt and black pepper
6	anchovy fillets, finely chopped	2	tablespoons small white pickled onions
8	ounces (250 g) canned		

1. Cook the rice in a large pot of salted, boiling water until tender, 30-40 minutes.

2. Drain well and leave in the colander to cool for 5-10 minutes. Transfer the rice to a large bowl.

3. Combine the oil and lemon juice in a medium bowl. Add the egg yolk and use a fork to crush it into the oil mixture. Add the anchovies and beat with the fork until they dissolve into the mixture.

4. Add the tuna, capers, olives, pickled onions, and gherkins to the oil and anchovies mixture. Season with salt and pepper.

5. Spoon this mixture over the rice, toss gently, and serve.

high protein salads

WARM STICKY PORK with pineapple salsa

Sticky Pork Chops

4	(7-ounce/200-g) boneless pork chops
	Freshly ground sea salt and black pepper
1	cup (250 ml) pineapple juice
1/4	cup (60 ml) dark rum
2	tablespoons molasses
2	tablespoons sweet chili sauce
4	cloves garlic, minced
2	teaspoons minced fresh ginger
4	cups (200 g) fresh watercress

Pineapple Salsa

1	fresh sweet pineapple, peeled, core removed, and diced
2	tomatoes, diced
1	sweet red onion, diced
1	cup coarsely chopped fresh cilantro (coriander)
1	long red fresh chili, seeded and chopped
1	tablespoon extra-virgin olive oil
1/2	teaspoon ground cumin
1/2	teaspoon sea salt flakes

Serves 4 • Preparation 30 minutes + 2–12 hours to marinate • Cooking 15 minutes • Difficulty 1

Sticky Pork Chops

1. Season the pork chops with salt and pepper. Whisk the pineapple juice, rum, molasses, sweet chili sauce, garlic, and ginger in a bowl.

2. Place the pork chops in a shallow bowl and pour the marinade over the top, turning to coat. Chill for at least 2 hours, or overnight.

3. Preheat a grill pan (griddle) over medium-high heat.

4. Drain the marinade from the pork and pour into a pan. Bring to a boil then simmer until the mixture starts to look slightly shiny, about 5 minutes.

5. Grill the pork until cooked through but still moist, 4–5 minutes each side. Set aside for 5 minutes.

Pineapple Salsa

1. Combine all the salsa ingredients in a bowl and toss well to combine.

2. Arrange the pork chops, watercress, and salsa on serving plates. Drizzle with the reduced marinade, and serve warm.

Halloumi is an unripened brined cheese made from a mixture of goat's and sheep's milk originally from Cyprus. It has a high melting point and is especially good for grilling and frying.

GRILLED HALLOUMI with oranges, watercress & mint

3	medium oranges, segments and juice
1	small bunch coarsely chopped fresh mint leaves
1	tablespoon white wine vinegar
1/4	cup (60 ml) extra-virgin olive oil
	Freshly ground sea salt and black pepper
1	pound (500 g) halloumi cheese, drained and sliced into 15-20 pieces
1	cup (120 g) walnut pieces, toasted
6	cups (300 g) fresh watercress
	Pita bread, to serve

Serves 6 • Preparation 15 minutes • Cooking 15–20 minutes
Difficulty 1

1. Preheat a large grill pan (griddle) or frying pan over high heat.

2. Combine the segments of orange and juice, mint leaves, vinegar, and oil in a large bowl. Season with salt and pepper, and toss gently to mix.

3. Grill or fry the cheese on both sides until charred and beginning to melt, 2–3 minutes each side.

4. Add the walnuts and watercress to the orange salad, tossing well. Top with the halloumi and season with black pepper.

5. Serve warm, with the pita bread

If you liked this recipe, you will love these as well.

WARM STICKY PORK
with pineapple salsa

MACKEREL
with couscous

LENTIL & HALLOUMI
salad

SHRIMP & MANGO salad

Salad

2	mangoes, peeled and pitted
4	scallions (spring onions), sliced on the diagonal
8	ounces (250 g) cooked shrimp (prawns), peeled and deveined
4	cups (200 g) baby spinach leaves

Dressing

$1/2$	cup (125 ml) plain yogurt
$1/4$	cup (60 ml) mango chutney

Serves 4 • Preparation 15 minutes • Difficulty 1

Salad

1. Working over a bowl to catch any juice, cut the mangoes into thin slices.

2. Mix the mangoes, scallions, and shrimp in a medium bowl.

3. Arrange the spinach leaves on four individual serving plates. Top with the shrimp mixture.

Dressing

1. Whisk the yogurt, mango chutney, and reserved mango juice in a medium bowl until well combined.

2. Drizzle the dressing over the salads, and serve.

BACON & EGG salad

Salad

6   cups (300 g) mixed salad greens
1   tablespoon finely chopped fresh chives
1   red bell pepper (capsicum), seeded and very thinly sliced
6   slices baguette (French loaf), toasted, rubbed with garlic, and cut into squares
6   large thick slices bacon, rinds removed
1   tablespoon vinegar
6   large eggs
    Freshly ground black pepper

Dressing

2   tablespoons red wine vinegar
1   teaspoon balsamic vinegar
    Salt
1   teaspoon Dijon mustard
1   clove garlic, finely chopped
1/3 cup (90 ml) extra-virgin olive oil

Serves 6 • Preparation 15 minutes • Cooking 10 minutes • Difficulty 1

Salad

1. Combine the salad greens, chives, bell pepper, and toasted squares of bread in a large bowl.

2. Dry-fry the bacon in a frying pan until crisp and golden, about 5 minutes. Drain on paper towels. Cut into thin strips.

3. Fill a lidded frying pan with water, and bring to a boil. Add the vinegar. Break the eggs into a cup one at a time, then pour into the pan. Turn off the heat under the pan and cover tightly. Set aside for 4 minutes.

4. Place a clean cloth next to the pan and, using a slotted spoon, carefully scoop out the eggs and place on the cloth.

Dressing

1. Whisk the dressing ingredients in a small bowl.

2. Drizzle the dressing over the salad and toss gently. Divide among six serving plates. Top each one with an egg and some bacon. Season with pepper, and serve.

This salad is perfect for special occasions. It is also convenient because it can be prepared in advance and chilled until just before serving.

SEAFOOD salad

1	pound (500 g) mussels, in shell
1	pound (500 g) medium shrimp (prawns), peeled and deveined
2	pounds (1 kg) fresh, cleaned squid (calamari), cut into $^1/_2$-inch (1-cm) rings, leaving tentacles whole
8	ounces (250 g) fresh shucked scallops, roe removed
2	tablespoons butter
2	stalks celery, sliced
1	medium red onion, sliced
1	(8-ounce/250-g) jar roasted red bell peppers (capsicums), drained and diced
$^1/_2$	cup (120 ml) extra-virgin olive oil
$^1/_2$	cup (120 ml) freshly squeezed lemon juice
4	cloves garlic, minced
	Small bunch coarsely chopped fresh parsley
	Freshly ground sea salt and black pepper
	Freshly baked focaccia or crusty ciabatta bread, to serve

Serves 6–8 • Preparation 45 minutes + 1 hour to soak & 4–12 hours to chill • Cooking 15–20 minutes • Difficulty 2

1. Soak the mussels in cold water for 1 hour. Scrub with a stiff brush under cold running water. Remove any beards from mussels and discard any with broken or open shells.

2. Put 1 tablespoon of water in a large saucepan and add the mussels. Cover and cook over high heat until the mussels open, 3–5 minutes. Discard any mussels that do not open. Transfer to a bowl and let cool.

3. Bring a large pot of salted water to a boil over high heat. Set a bowl of ice water nearby. Boil the shrimp until pink, about 2 minutes. Remove with tongs and set aside.

4. Add half the squid to the boiling water and return to a boil. Cook until opaque, about 1 minute. Drain well, pat dry with paper towels, and add to the bowl of shrimp. Repeat with the remaining squid.

5. Heat the butter in a small frying pan over medium heat and cook the scallops until opaque, 2–3 minutes. Set aside to cool a little.

6. Strain the liquid off the mussels and add to the bowl of squid and shrimp. Add the scallops, onion, celery, and bell peppers to the bowl.

7. Whisk the oil, lemon juice, garlic, parsley, salt and pepper in a bowl until well combined.

8. Pour the dressing over the salad, tossing gently. Cover with plastic wrap (cling film) and chill for 4 hours, or overnight.

9. Let sit at room temperature for 30 minutes before serving.

WARM SALMON & POTATO salad

2   large red bell peppers (capsicums), halved and seeded

4   tablespoons (60 ml) extra-virgin olive oil + extra, to brush

4   salmon fillets, skin on

3   tablespoons pine nuts

1   pound (500 g) small new potatoes

1   tablespoon balsamic vinegar

3   ounces (90 g) marinated anchovies

2   tablespoons capers, rinsed

$1/2$ cup fresh basil, shredded

2   cups (100 g) arugula (rocket)

Serves 4 • Preparation 20 minutes • Cooking 25–30 minutes • Difficulty 2

1. Preheat the oven to 425°F (220°C/gas 7).

2. Brush the bell peppers with a little oil, then place, skin-side up, in a large roasting pan. Roast for 15 minutes, then add the salmon to the pan, skin–side down. Sprinkle with the pine nuts and return to the oven for 10 more minutes.

3. Boil the potatoes in their skins until tender, 8–10 minutes. Thickly slice or halve, depending on their size.

4. Whisk the 4 tablespoons of oil with the vinegar in a large bowl. Add the anchovies and capers.

5. When the peppers are cool enough to handle, peel off the skins, and cut the flesh into long thin strips. Toss in the oil mixture with the basil and potatoes, adding any cooking juices from the baking pan.

6. Transfer to a large platter with the arugula. Flake the salmon on top in chunky pieces and sprinkle with the roasted pine nuts. Serve warm.

THAI SEAFOOD salad

Vinaigrette

3	small red Thai chilies, seeded and minced
1	tablespoon Asian fish sauce
1	tablespoon sugar
1/3	cup (90 ml) peanut oil
1/4	cup finely chopped lemongrass
1/4	cup (60 ml) freshly squeezed lime juice

Salad

12	ounces (350 g) whole squid (calamari) bodies, cleaned
12	ounces (350 g) shrimp (prawns), deveined and shelled
12	ounces (350 g) baby octopus, cleaned and halved lengthwise
1	large mango, peeled, pitted and cubed
4	cups (200 g) watercress
24	cherry tomatoes, halved
1	cup Thai basil leaves, torn
1/2	cup fresh cilantro (coriander)
	Freshly ground sea salt and black pepper

Serves 4–6 • Preparation 30 minutes • Cooking 10–15 minutes
Difficulty 1

Vinaigrette

1. Whisk all the vinaigrette ingredients together in a small bow and set aside.

Salad

1. Cut each squid open lengthwise, without cutting it in half, so you can open it up and lay it flat. Score it with a knife in a diamond pattern, then cut the body into bite-size squares or rectangles. This will help the squid lay flat while grilling.

2. Combine all the seafood in a bowl with half the dressing and marinate for two hours.

3. Combine the mango, watercress, tomatoes, basil, and cilantro in a large bowl.

4. Preheat a large grill pan (griddle) or chargrill over medium-high heat. Grill the seafood in two or three batches, about 5 minutes each batch. Cool the seafood for a few minutes before mixing it into the salad.

5. Dress with the remaining vinaigrette, season with salt and pepper, and serve.

CHICKEN & WALNUT salad

Serves 4 • Preparation 15 minutes + 15 minutes to soak
Cooking 10–15 minutes • Difficulty 1

Salad

4	boneless, skinless chicken breast halves		cheese, crumbled
	Pinch of mixed herbs	2	cups (100 g) spinach
1	teaspoon sea salt flakes		**Dressing**
1	pear, cored and thinly sliced, drizzled with 1 tablespoon lemon juice	1/2	cup (120 ml) extra-virgin olive oil
1/2	cup (60 g) walnuts	2	tablespoons fresh lemon juice
4	ounces (120 g) blue	1	clove garlic, minced
			Salt and freshly ground black pepper

Salad

1. Bring 3 cups (750 ml) of water to a boil and add the mixed herbs, salt, and chicken. Simmer until tender, 10–15 minutes. Let sit in the cooking water for 15 minutes. Drain well and set aside to cool.

2. Cut the chicken into 1/2-inch (1-cm) thick slices.

3. Toss the chicken, walnuts, pear, blue cheese, and spinach in a salad bowl.

Dressing

1. Whisk all the ingredients in a small bowl. Drizzle over the salad, and serve.

SALMON SALAD with beets

Serves 4 • Preparation 15 minutes • Cooking 15 minutes
Difficulty 1

Salad

4	large potatoes, with skin, thickly sliced	4	cups (200 g) watercress
2	cups (300 g) frozen peas	6	scallions (spring onions), sliced
4	slices lean bacon, rinds removed		**Dressing**
6	(5-ounce/150-g) salmon fillets, skinned	1/3	cup (90 ml) extra-virgin olive oil
12	ounces (350 g) cooked beets (beetroot)	3	tablespoons freshly squeezed lemon juice
		1	teaspoon Dijon mustard
			Freshly ground sea salt and black pepper

Salad

1. Boil the potatoes in salted water until tender, 10–12 minutes, adding the peas for the final 3–4 minutes. Drain and let cool.

2. Dry-fry the bacon in a large frying pan over medium heat until golden, about 5 minutes. Scoop out and set aside. Add the salmon to the pan and fry until golden, 2–3 minutes each side.

Dressing

1. Whisk all the ingredients in a small bowl.

2. Put the potatoes, peas, beets, and salad on plates. Top with the salmon, bacon, and dressing, and serve.

CHICKEN & ARUGULA salad

Serves 4 • Preparation 15 minutes • Cooking 6–10 minutes
Difficulty 1

Dressing

1/3	cup (90 ml) freshly squeezed lemon juice		Freshly ground sea salt and black pepper
3	cloves garlic, minced		**Salad**
2	tablespoons coarsely chopped fresh basil	2	boneless skinless chicken breasts, sliced
1	tablespoon brown sugar	1	(14-ounce/400-g) can garbanzo beans (chickpeas), drained
1/2	cup (120 ml) extra-virgin olive oil	3	cups (150 g) arugula (rocket)

Dressing

1. Whisk the lemon juice, garlic, basil, brown sugar, and oil in a small bowl. Season with salt and pepper.

Salad

1. Heat a grill pan (griddle) or barbecue over high heat. Grill the chicken until tender and cooked through, 3–5 minutes each side. During cooking, turn the chicken and baste with half the dressing.

2. Put the garbanzo beans and arugula in a salad bowl. Drizzle with the remaining dressing and toss gently. Top with the chicken, toss a little, and serve.

MACKEREL with couscous

Serves 4 • Preparation 10 minutes + 10 minutes to soak
Difficulty 1

2	cups (300 g) quick whole-wheat (wholemeal) couscous		Freshly ground black pepper
3	oranges, 2 peeled and thinly sliced, 1 freshly juiced	1	red onion, finely chopped
3	tablespoons red wine vinegar	2	cups (100 g) arugula (rockets) leaves
1	teaspoon sugar	8	ounces (250 g) smoked mackerel, flaked into large chunks
3	tablespoons extra-virgin olive oil		

1. Pour 2 cups (500 ml) of boiling water over the couscous, cover, and leave to soak for 10 minutes.

2. Whisk the orange juice, vinegar, sugar, oil, and pepper in a small bowl.

3. Mix the orange juice mixture into the couscous. Add the oranges, onion, arugula, and mackerel. Toss gently, and serve.

If you can't get snow peas, replace them with watercress, arugula (rocket), or another salad green to your liking.

GRILLED CHICKEN SALAD
with olives, mint & yogurt

2 tablespoons plain yogurt

Freshly squeezed juice of 1 lemon

1 tablespoon dried oregano

2 tablespoons finely chopped fresh mint

1 pound (500 g) chicken tenderloins, trimmed

3 tablespoons extra-virgin olive oil + extra, to drizzle

3 cups (150 g) baby spinach leaves

5 ounces (150 g) roasted yellow bell pepper (capsicum), from a can or jar, drained and sliced

1 cucumber, coarsely chopped

1 cup (50 g) snow pea sprouts

4 ounces (120 g) feta cheese, crumbled

1/2 cup (50 g) kalamata olives

Freshly ground sea salt and black pepper

Serves 4-6 • Preparation 15 minutes • Cooking 15–20 minutes
Difficulty 1

1. Combine the yogurt, 2 teaspoons of the lemon juice, oregano, and mint in a bowl, mixing well. Add the chicken, turning to coat. Cover and chill in the refrigerator for 30 minutes.

2. Preheat a grill pan (griddle), overhead broiler (grill), or barbecue grill on medium heat. Remove the chicken from marinade and brush with the oil. Grill or broil until cooked through, 5–10 minutes, depending on the cooking method.

3. Combine the spinach, bell pepper, cucumber, snow pea sprouts, feta, and olives in a bowl. Toss to combine.

4. Divide the salad among four serving plates. Top each portion with a quarter of the chicken. Drizzle with remaining lemon juice and extra oil. Season with salt and pepper, and serve.

If you liked this recipe, you will love these as well.

CHICKEN & ARUGULA salad

HONEY & MUSTARD chicken salad

CHICKEN & GARBANZO BEAN salad

HONEY & MUSTARD chicken salad

Salad

1/4	cup (60 ml) clear honey
2	tablespoons wholegrain mustard
	Freshly ground sea salt and black pepper
4	boneless, skinless chicken breast halves, about 6 ounces (180 g) each
4	cups (200 g) mixed salad greens
20	cherry tomatoes, halved

Dressing

1/3	cup (90 ml) extra-virgin olive oil
2	tablespoons balsamic vinegar
	Freshly ground sea salt and black pepper

Serves 4 • Preparation 15 minutes • Cooking 5-10 minutes • Difficulty 1

Salad

1. Whisk the honey and mustard in a small bowl. Season with salt and pepper. Brush all over the chicken breasts.

2. Preheat a grill pan (griddle), overhead broiler (grill), or barbecue grill on medium heat. Grill or broil the chicken until cooked through and golden, 5-10 minutes, depending on the cooking method.

3. Let the chicken cool for 5 minutes, then slice.

4. Combine the salad greens and cherry tomatoes in a bowl. Toss well then divide equally among four serving plates. Top each portion with a quarter of the chicken.

Dressing

1. Whisk the oil and balsamic vinegar in a small bowl. Season with salt and pepper. Drizzle over the salads, and serve.

GRILLED DUCK BREAST salad

Salad

1¹/₂   pounds (750 g) boneless duck breasts, skin on

Freshly ground sea salt and black pepper

4   cups (200 g) mixed arugula and watercress salad greens

24   cherry tomatoes, halved

6   scallions (spring onions), sliced diagonally

Dressing

2   cloves garlic, minced

2   teaspoons finely grated ginger

¹/₄   cup (60 ml) soy sauce

¹/₃   cup (90 ml) honey

Serves 4-6 • Preparation 15 minutes • Cooking 20–30 minutes
Difficulty 2

Salad

1. Preheat the oven to 400°F (200°C/gas 6). Score the skin on the duck breasts and season with salt and pepper.

2. Heat a frying pan over high heat. Add the duck, skin-side down, and cook until the skin is crisp, 4–5 minutes. Turn over and brown the underside. Transfer to a baking sheet.

Dressing

1. Whisk the garlic, ginger, soy sauce, and honey in a bowl.

2. Spoon all but 2 tablespoons of the dressing over the duck. Roast until cooked to your liking (10 minutes for pink, longer if you prefer it well done.)

3. Remove the duck from the oven and set aside to rest for 5 minutes. Slice into strips.

4. Combine the salad greens, cherry tomatoes, scallions, and duck in a salad bowl. Toss gently. Drizzle with the remaining dressing, and serve.

This is a very light and healthy salad, perfect for lunch or a light dinner.

CHICKEN & GARBANZO BEAN salad

1¼	pounds (600 g) boneless skinless chicken breast fillets
5	tablespoons (75 ml) extra-virgin olive oil
1	tablespoon freshly ground black pepper
1	tablespoon sea salt flakes
1	(14-ounce/400-g) can fava beans (chickpeas), drained and rinsed
1	medium avocado, peeled, pitted, halved, and thinly sliced
2	cups (100 g) arugula (rocket)
1	small red onion, halved, thinly sliced
12	cherry tomatoes, halved
2	tablespoons coarsely chopped fresh basil
2	tablespoons freshly squeezed lime juice
1	clove garlic, minced

Serves 4–6 • Preparation 15 minutes • Cooking 10 minutes
Difficulty 1

1. Preheat a grill pan (griddle) or chargrill on medium-high heat. Place the chicken in a bowl and brush with 1–2 tablespoons of the oil. Season with the salt and pepper, turning to coat.

2. Grill until browned and cooked through, about 5 minutes each side. Transfer to a plate. Cover with foil and set aside for 5 minutes to rest. Slice across the grain into ½-inch (1-cm) thick pieces.

3. Combine the fava beans, avocado, arugula, onion, cherry tomatoes, basil, and chicken in a bowl.

4. Whisk the remaining oil, lime juice, and garlic in a small bowl. Pour over salad. Toss to combine, and serve.

If you liked this recipe, you will love these as well.

GRILLED CHICKEN SALAD with olives, mint & yogurt

SPICY CHICKEN SALAD with apple

WARM CHICKEN & GOAT CHEESE salad

CHICKEN & MANGO salad

6	shallots, halved
2	small red chilies, 1 whole and 1 finely chopped
1	tablespoon grated ginger
	Finely grated zest and juice of 1 unwaxed lime
1	tablespoon sunflower oil
	Freshly ground sea salt and black pepper
2	boneless chicken breasts, skin on
1	organic red apple, with peel, cut into matchsticks
1/2	mango, peeled and cut into matchsticks
1	small bunch fresh mint leaves
3	scallions (spring onions), sliced
	Small bunch fresh cilantro (coriander)
1/2	teaspoon Thai fish sauce + extra, as required
1/4	teaspoon sugar

Serves 4 • Preparation 30 minutes • Cooking 20–25 minutes • Difficulty 2

1. Finely chop the shallots in a food processor. Add the whole chili, three-quarters of the ginger, and all the lime zest. Chop to a chunky paste. Add to a frying pan with the oil, season with salt and pepper, and sauté until fragrant, 1–2 minutes. Set aside.

2. Preheat the oven to 400°F (200°C/gas 6). Cut the skin from the chicken breasts along one side, and stuff with the shallot mixture. Season with salt and pepper. Place in a roasting pan and roast for 15–20 minutes, until golden and cooked. Set aside to cool, then tear into bite-size pieces.

3. Toss the apple, mango, mint, scallions, and half the cilantro in a bowl. Mix in the fish sauce, sugar, remaining ginger, and lime juice, and set aside.

4. Put the roasting pan on the stove top. Spoon off any excess fat, then gently heat, adding 1–2 teaspoons of fish sauce and scraping up the juices. Chop the remaining cilantro. Stir into the sauce with the chopped chili.

5. Toss the salad with the chicken and dressing, and serve warm.

SPICY CHICKEN SALAD with apple

2	stalks lemongrass, chopped
4	lime leaves, chopped
2	fresh red chilies, seeded and chopped
3	cloves garlic, chopped
1	(1-inch/2.5-cm) piece ginger, peeled
2	tablespoons sesame oil
4	boneless skinless chicken breast halves
1	teaspoon chili powder
1/4	cup (60 ml) Thai fish sauce
1	red onion, chopped
2	romaine (cos) lettuces, thickly sliced
1	cucumber, thinly sliced lengthwise
1	cup (50 g) bean sprouts
2	stalks celery, sliced
1	green apple, peeled and cut into chunks
3	tablespoons freshly squeezed lime juice
1	tablespoon fresh mint
1	tablespoon fresh basil
1	tablespoon fresh cilantro (coriander)

Serves 4 • Preparation 30 minutes • Cooking 10–15 minutes • Difficulty 2

1. Combine the lemongrass, lime leaves, chilies, garlic, and ginger in a food processor and chop finely.

2. Heat a wok over high heat and add the oil. Add the lemongrass mixture and stir-fry for 1 minute. Add the chicken and chili powder and stir-fry for 4 minutes.

3. Add the fish sauce. Decrease the heat to medium and let the chicken and fish sauce bubble for 5 minutes, stirring often. Add the onion and stir-fry for 1 minute. Remove from the heat.

4. Spread the lettuce, cucumber, bean sprouts, celery, and apple on a serving platter or individual serving plates. Top with the chicken mixture. Drizzle with the lime juice and sprinkle with the mint, basil, and cilantro. Serve warm.

For a dish lower in fat and calories, use skinned chicken breasts.

WARM CHICKEN & GOAT CHEESE salad

4	boneless chicken breasts, with skin, cut into bite-size pieces
1	baguette (French loaf), broken into bite-size chunks
1	teaspoon dried oregano
	Freshly ground sea salt and black pepper
$^1/_2$	cup (120 ml) extra-virgin olive oil
2	tablespoons balsamic vinegar
1	clove garlic, minced
6	cups (300 g) mixed salad greens
24	cherry tomatoes, halved
5	ounces (150 g) goat cheese

Serves 4 • Preparation 15 minutes • Cooking 15–20 minutes
Difficulty 1

1. Preheat the oven to 400°F (200°C/gas 6).

2. Spread the chicken and bread out in a large shallow roasting pan. Dust with the oregano and season with salt and pepper. Drizzle with half the oil, tossing to coat.

3. Bake for 15–20 minutes, until the chicken is cooked through and the bread is golden and crisp.

4. Whisk the remaining oil with the balsamic vinegar and garlic to make a dressing.

5. Combine the salad greens and tomatoes in a bowl. Drizzle with the dressing, tossing to coat.

6. Arrange the salad on four serving plates. Top with the chicken and goat cheese, and serve warm.

If you liked this recipe, you will love these as well.

CHICKEN & WALNUT
salad

LEBANESE CHICKEN
salad

GRILLED CHICKEN,
ORANGE & COUSCOUS
salad

LEBANESE CHICKEN salad

Salad

1	cup (180 g) bulgur
2	cups (500 ml) boiling water
1	ready-roasted or barbecued chicken
4	ounces (120 g) roasted red bell pepper (capsicum), from a can or jar, drained and thinly sliced
1	small red onion, thinly sliced
1	(14-ounce/400-g) can garbanzo beans (chickpeas), drained and rinsed
2	cups (100 g) finely chopped fresh parsley
1	cup (50 g) finely chopped fresh mint

Dressing

1/4	cup (60 ml) extra-virgin olive oil
1/3	cup (90 ml) freshly squeezed lemon juice
	Freshly ground sea salt and black pepper

Serves 4 • Preparation 20 minutes + 10 minutes to soak • Difficulty 1

Salad

1. Place the bulgur in a heatproof bowl and pour in the boiling water. Stir to combine. Set aside for 10 minutes. Drain well, pressing to remove as much of the liquid as possible. Transfer the bulgur to a large salad bowl.

2. Remove the flesh from the chicken. Discard the skin and bones. Shred the chicken flesh.

3. Add the chicken flesh, bell pepper, onion, garbanzo beans, parsley, and mint to the bowl with the bulgur.

Dressing

1. Whisk the oil and lemon juice in a small bowl. Season with salt and pepper.

2. Drizzle the dressing over the salad, toss gently, and serve.

SPRING CHICKEN salad

Salad

1	ready-roasted or barbecued chicken
3	cups (150 g) baby spinach leaves
1	large carrot, peeled, thinly sliced
4	scallions (spring onions), thinly sliced
2	bunches asparagus, trimmed, cut into thirds
3	tablespoons sesame seeds, toasted

Dressing

$1/3$	cup (90 ml) freshly squeezed orange juice
2	tablespoons tahini
	Freshly ground sea salt and black pepper

Serves 4 • Preparation 20 minutes • Cooking 2–3 minutes • Difficulty 1

Salad

1. Remove the flesh from the chicken. Discard the skin and bones. Shred the chicken.

2. Combine the chicken, spinach, carrot, and scallions in a large salad bowl.

3. Half-fill a frying pan with water. Bring to a boil over medium heat. Add the asparagus. Cook until just tender, 2–3 minutes, depending on the thickness of the stalks.

4. Drain well and set aside to cool a little.

Dressing

1. Whisk the orange juice and tahini in a small bowl. Season with salt and pepper.

2. Add the asparagus to the chicken mixture. Drizzle with the dressing and toss to combine. Sprinkle with the sesame seeds, and serve.

This hearty salad is great in the winter, when oranges are in season.

GRILLED CHICKEN, ORANGE & COUSCOUS salad

4	small boneless skinless chicken breasts, cut into bite-size pieces
5	tablespoons (75 ml) extra-virgin olive oil
	Freshly ground sea salt and black pepper
1$\frac{1}{2}$	cups (250 g) couscous
	Freshly squeezed juice of 2 lemons
4	oranges, 2 juiced, 2 left whole, peeled and cut into bite-size pieces
1	teaspoon ground cumin
1	clove garlic, minced
1	cup chopped fresh basil
1	cup chopped fresh cilantro (coriander)
1	cup (120 g) roasted salted peanuts
4	cups (200 g) watercress

Serves 4 • Preparation 15 minutes + 25 minutes to soak • Cooking 10–15 minutes • Difficulty 1

1. Preheat a grill pan (griddle) over medium-high heat. Drizzle the chicken with 2 tablespoons of the oil and season with salt and pepper. Grill the until cooked through and brown on the outside, 10–15 minutes.

2. Put the couscous in a bowl and pour in enough boiling water to cover by about 1 inch (2.5 cm). Set aside to soak for 15 minutes, until the couscous has absorbed the liquid

3. Whisk the lemon and orange juice with the cumin, garlic, and remaining 3 tablespoons of oil. Season with salt and pepper. Pour over the couscous and let soak for 10 minutes.

4. Add the orange chunks, chicken, basil, cilantro, peanuts, and watercress to the couscous in the bowl, mix well, and serve.

If you liked this recipe, you will love these as well.

CHICKEN & MANGO
salad

SPICY CHICKEN SALAD
with apple

THAI CHICKEN
salad

ASIAN CHICKEN salad

Salad

1	(4-pound/2-g) chicken
1	onion, quartered
2	kaffir lime (or bay) leaves
2	stalks lemongrass, bruised
1	cucumber, peeled, cut horizontally into long strips
1	teaspoon sea salt flakes
4	tablespoons white sesame seeds
3	stalks celery, sliced
2	large carrots, peeled and cut into long thin strips
2	cups (100 g) finely shredded white cabbage
1/2	cup fresh mint
1/2	cup fresh cilantro (coriander)
4-6	cos or romaine lettuce leaves
	Freshly ground black pepper
1	cup (120 g) toasted cashews

Dressing

2	cloves garlic, minced
1	red chili, seeded and chopped
3	tablespoons brown sugar
2	limes
3	tablespoons Thai fish sauce

Serves 4-6 • Preparation 15 minutes + 2-3 hours to cool • Cooking 1 hour • Difficulty 1

Salad

1. Put the chicken in a stockpot with the onion, kaffir lime leaves, and lemongrass. Add water to cover, bring to a boil, and simmer for 1 hour. Let cool in the liquid, 2-3 hours.

2. Drain, discard the skin, pull the flesh off the bones and tear into bite-sized pieces. Place in a bowl and set aside.

3. Put the cucumber in a bowl and sprinkle with salt. Set aside for 10 minutes.

4. Dry-fry the sesame seeds in a small frying pan over medium heat until golden. Set aside.

5. Squeeze the cucumber to remove excess liquid. Place in a bowl. Add the celery, carrots, cabbage, chicken, and most of the sesame seeds, reserving a few to garnish.

Dressing

1. Whisk all the dressing ingredients in a small bowl.

2. Toss the salad with the dressing, mint, and cilantro. Line a serving plate with the lettuce. Pile the salad on top and sprinkle with the remaining sesame and the cashews, and serve warm.

THAI CHICKEN salad

Curry Paste

4	fresh red chilies
2	leeks, finely chopped
8	cloves garlic, chopped
1	bunch cilantro (coriander)
	Zest of 2 limes
2	teaspoons ground cumin
2	teaspoons Thai fish sauce

Salad

2	tablespoons peanut oil
1½	pounds (600 g) ground (minced) chicken
	Freshly ground sea salt and black pepper
2	mangos, peeled, pitted, and sliced
2	fresh red chilies, sliced
3	cloves garlic, sliced
2	cos gem lettuces, coarsely chopped
½	cup each fresh cilantro (coriander), basil, and mint

Dressing

	Freshly squeezed juice of 3 limes
1	tablespoon brown sugar
1	tablespoon soy sauce
2	tablespoons sesame oil

Serves 4–6 • Preparation 30 minutes • Cooking 7–10 minutes
Difficulty 2

Curry Paste

1. Blend all of the curry paste ingredients in a food processor.

Salad

1. Heat the oil in a wok over medium-high heat. Add the chicken, season with salt and pepper, and stir-fry until golden and becoming crisp, 7–10 minutes.
2. Add four tablespoons of the curry paste. Stir well to heat through. Set aside.
3. Combine the mangos, chilies, garlic, lettuce, and herbs in a large bowl, tossing gently but well.

Dressing

1. Whisk all the dressing ingredients together in a bowl.
2. Toss the dressing with the chicken, and serve on the salad.

This hearty dish makes a great family dinner or can be served to friends when entertaining casually.

STEAK SALAD
with onion rings & candied walnuts

Steak

3/4	cup (180 ml) extra-virgin olive oil
3	tablespoons red wine vinegar
1	tablespoon balsamic vinegar
1	tablespoon Worcestershire sauce
2	tablespoons soy sauce + 1 teaspoon
2	tablespoons fresh lime juice
2	tablespoons brown sugar
4	cloves garlic
2	teaspoons minced ginger
1	teaspoon hot chili paste
1	teaspoon sea salt flakes
	Freshly ground black pepper
2	rib-eye steaks

Onion Rings

2	onions, thinly sliced
2	cups (500 ml) buttermilk
2	cups (300 g) all-purpose (plain) flour
1	teaspoon sea salt flakes
4	cups (1 liter) canola oil

Candied Walnuts

1	cup (200 g) sugar
2	tablespoons water
1	cup (120 g) walnut halves

Salad

4	cups (200 g) salad greens
4	ounces (120 g) blue cheese, such as Gorgonzola, Danish, Stilton or Roquefort, crumbled
20	cherry tomatoes, halved

Serves 4 • Preparation 30 minutes + 2 hours to chill • Cooking 15–20 minutes • Difficulty 2

Steaks

1. Whisk all the steak ingredients except the steaks in a bowl.

2. Put the steaks in a bowl. Pour in half the marinade and cover with plastic wrap (cling film). Chill for at least two hours. Chill the remaining marinade until ready to serve.

Onion Rings

1. Place the onions in a baking dish and cover with buttermilk. Soak for at least 1 hour.

2. Combine the flour and salt in a bowl. Heat the oil in a deep fryer to 375°F (180°C). Toss the onions in the flour mixture and fry in batches until golden, 3–5 minutes each batch. Scoop out with a slotted spoon and drain on paper towels.

Candied Walnuts

1. Combine the sugar and water in a small frying pan over medium heat. Simmer until deep amber in color, about 5 minutes. Add the walnuts, stirring to coat evenly. Pour onto a plate lined with parchment paper and let cool.

Salad

1. Preheat a grill pan (griddle) over medium-high heat. Drain the marinade from the steak. Discard the marinade. Grill the steaks until medium-rare, 3–4 minutes on each side. Let rest for 5 minutes the slice thinly against the grain.

2. Combine the salad greens, cheese, and tomatoes in a bowl. Add half the dressing and toss to combine. Add the candied walnuts and toss to combine.

3. Heap onto serving plates. Top with steak and onion rings. Drizzle with the remaining marinade, and serve hot.

STEAK, AVOCADO & TORTILLA salad

5	tablespoons extra-virgin olive oil
4	(5-ounce/150-g) sirloin steaks, trimmed of any fat
	Freshly ground sea salt and black pepper
2	tablespoons balsamic vinegar
1	teaspoon Dijon mustard
1	clove garlic, minced
4	cups (200 g) mixed salad greens
20	cherry tomatoes, halved
2	avocados, peeled, pitted, and thickly sliced
1	(12-ounce/350-g) package tortilla chips
1	cup fresh cilantro (coriander)

Serves 4 • Preparation 15 minutes • Cooking 6–8 minutes • Difficulty 1

1. Rub 2 tablespoons of oil over the steaks and season with salt and pepper. Preheat a large grill pan (griddle) over medium-high heat.

2. Grill the steaks until cooked to your liking, 3–4 minutes each side for medium-rare. Remove from the pan and set aside on a plate while you prepare the other ingredients.

3. Whisk the remaining 3 tablespoons of oil, vinegar, mustard, garlic, and the resting juices from the steak in a small bowl.

4. Slice the steaks thinly against the grain.

5. Combine the salad greens, cherry tomatoes, avocados, tortilla chips, and cilantro in a bowl, tossing to coat. Divide the salad evenly among four serving plates. Top with the steak, drizzle with the dressing, and serve warm.

STEAK SALAD
with grilled onions & blue cheese

1 teaspoon Worcestershire sauce

6 tablespoons (90 ml) extra-virgin olive oil

1 pound (500 g) skirt steak, trimmed and cut in half

4 teaspoons red wine vinegar

1 teaspoon Dijon mustard

1 teaspoon honey

2 cloves garlic, minced

Freshly ground sea salt and black pepper

1 large red onion, sliced

6 cups (250 g) mixed baby salad greens

20 cherry tomatoes, halved

3½ ounces (100 g) blue cheese, such as Gorgonzola, Danish, Stilton or Roquefort, crumbled

Serves 4 • Preparation 15 minutes • Cooking 10 minutes • Difficulty 1

1. Preheat a large grill pan (griddle) over medium-high heat.

2. Combine the Worcestershire sauce and 1 tablespoon of oil in a baking dish just large enough to hold the steak. Add the steak, turning to coat.

3. Combine the vinegar, mustard, honey, garlic, salt, and pepper in a bowl. Slowly whisk in the 4 tablespoons of oil.

4. Brush the onion with the remaining 1 tablespoon of oil, and grill until tender, 3–4 minutes. Season the steak with salt and pepper and grill with the onion, for 3–4 minutes each side for medium-rare. Let rest for 5 minutes.

5. Toss the salad greens and tomatoes with half the dressing and divide among four serving plates. Slice the steak across the grain, separate the onion into rings, and arrange both over the salad. Sprinkle with the blue cheese, drizzle with the remaining dressing, and serve warm.

THAI BEEF salads

Serves 4 • Preparation 15 minutes • Cooking 6–8 minutes
Difficulty 2

1	pound (500 g) boned rump steak, trimmed	¼	Chinese or napa cabbage, shredded
	Freshly ground sea salt and black pepper	¼	cup fresh cilantro (coriander) leaves
1	small fresh red chili, finely chopped	1	cup fresh mint
2	tablespoons freshly squeezed lime juice	4	ounces (120 g) snow peas (mangetout),
2	tablespoons Thai fish sauce	1	cucumber, thinly sliced
2	tablespoons brown sugar	1	small red onion, thinly sliced
1	teaspoon sesame oil	16	cherry tomatoes, halved

1. Heat a grill pan over medium-high heat. Season the steak with salt and pepper. Grill the steak until cooked to your liking; 3–4 minutes each side for medium-rare. Remove and slice across the grain.

2. Whisk the chili, lime juice, fish sauce, sugar, and sesame oil in a small bowl.

3. Combine the cabbage, half the cilantro, mint, snow peas, cucumber, onion, and tomatoes on a large serving plate. Top with the steak and dressing. Garnish with the remaining cilantro, and serve.

SAUSAGE salad

Serves 4 • Preparation 15 minutes • Cooking 12–15 minutes
Difficulty 1

1	tablespoon extra-virgin olive oil	1	tablespoon brown sugar
14	ounces (400 g) highly flavored, good quality pork sausages, sliced	16	cherry tomatoes, halved
		2	romaine (cos) lettuces
		1	large avocado, peeled, pitted, and sliced
1	red onion, coarsely chopped	1	small cucumber, sliced
2	tablespoons wholegrain mustard	1	tablespoon red wine vinegar
		1	tablespoon water

1. Heat the oil in a large frying pan over medium-high heat. Add the sausages and onion and sauté until golden brown, 8–10 minutes.

2. Add the mustard and sugar to the pan. Stir in the tomatoes and simmer until softening and coated in the mustard glaze, 4–5 minutes.

3. Combine the lettuce leaves, avocado, and cucumber in a bowl and toss gently. Arrange on a large serving platter. Spoon the hot sausage mixture on top.

4. Add the vinegar and water to the pan, stirring over medium heat with a wooden spoon to dislodge all the pan juices. Spoon over the salad, and serve.

GRILLED LAMB salad

Serves 6 • Preparation 20 minutes • Cooking 10 minutes
Difficulty 1

1	bunch asparagus, trimmed and cut into short lengths		seeds
		2	tablespoons red wine vinegar
1	cup (150 g) frozen peas	3	tomatoes, sliced
1	cup (150 g) fava (broad) beans		Freshly ground sea salt and black pepper
6	tablespoons (90 ml) extra-virgin olive oil		Handful fresh tarragon
			Handful fresh mint
1	tablespoon coriander	6	large lamb chops

1. Cook the asparagus, peas, and fava beans in a pan of salted, boiling water until just tender, 2–3 minutes. Drain well. Transfer to a bowl.

2. Heat the oil and coriander in a small saucepan over medium heat until fragrant, 1–2 minutes. Stir into the vegetables, with the vinegar, and tomatoes. Season with salt and pepper. Stir in the tarragon and mint.

3. Preheat a grill pan (griddle) on medium heat. Grill the lamb chops until cooked to your liking, 4–5 minutes on each side for medium-rare.

4. Place a chop on each of four serving plates, spoon the vegetable mixture over the top, and serve warm.

CHORIZO & EGG salad

Serves 4 • Preparation 20 minutes • Cooking 15–20 minutes
Difficulty 1

2	large sweet potatoes, skin on, sliced on the diagonal	1	clove garlic, minced
			Freshly squeezed juice of ½ lemon
5	ounces (150 g) chorizo, thinly sliced	3	cups (150 g) mixed salad leaves
4	tablespoons (60 ml) extra-virgin olive oil	20	cherry tomatoes, halved
	Freshly ground sea salt and black pepper	4	hard-boiled eggs, halved

1. Cook the sweet potatoes in a pan of salted boiling water until just tender. Drain and transfer to a bowl.

2. Heat a grill pan (griddle) until very hot. Toss the sweet potato and chorizo in 1 tablespoon of oil and season with salt and pepper. Grill until marked with lines. Return the sweet potatoes to the bowl. Grill the chorizo until crisp. Add to the bowl, leaving the juices behind.

3. Remove the pan from the heat. Add the garlic and remaining oil, and sizzle for 30 seconds. Add the lemon juice.

4. Arrange the salad and tomatoes on a serving plate, top with the sweet potatoes, eggs, and chorizo. Drizzle with the hot dressing, and serve.

Serve this salad with plenty of freshly baked bread to mop up the delicious juices.

GRILLED PORK SALAD
with raspberries & blue cheese

1	red onion, finely chopped
2	tablespoons balsamic vinegar
2	tablespoons finely chopped fresh parsley
	Freshly ground sea salt and black pepper
$1/3$	cup (90 ml) extra-virgin olive oil
4	(5-ounce/150-g) boneless pork chops
4	cups (200 g) salad greens
5	ounces (150 g) blue cheese, such as Gorgonzola, Danish, Stilton, or Roquefort, crumbled
1	cup (150 g) fresh raspberries

Serves 4 • Preparation 15 minutes + 15 minutes to marinate • Cooking 8–10 minutes • Difficulty 2

1. Combine the onion, vinegar, and 1 tablespoon of parsley in a medium bowl. Season with salt and pepper and whisk in the oil.

2. Put the pork chops in a shallow dish and season with salt. Add the remaining parsley and 3 tablespoons of the dressing. Turn the pork to coat and set aside to marinate for 15 minutes.

3. Preheat a grill pan (griddle) over medium-high heat. Grill the pork until cooked through but still moist, 4–5 minutes each side. Set aside to rest for 5 minutes.

4. Arrange the salad greens on a large serving platter. Top with the pork and sprinkle with the cheese and raspberries. Drizzle with the remaining dressing. Sprinkle with the remaining parsley, and serve warm.

If you liked this recipe, you will love these as well.

WARM STICKY PORK
with pineapple salsa

SAUSAGE
salad

CHORIZO & EGG
salad

superfood salads

CHEESE, WALNUT & BLUEBERRY salad

Salad

1	cup (120 g) walnut halves
8	cups (400 g) mixed salad greens
2	cups (300 g) fresh blueberries
5	ounces (150 g) blue cheese, such as Gorgonzola, Danish, Stilton or Roquefort, crumbled
$1/2$	cup coarsely chopped fresh parsley

Vinaigrette

$1/3$	cup (90 ml) extra-virgin olive oil
2	tablespoons apple cider vinegar
1	clove garlic, minced
	Freshly ground sea salt and black pepper

Serves 4 • Preparation 15 minutes • Cooking 3–4 minutes • Difficulty 1

Salad

1. Dry-fry the walnuts in a small frying pan over medium heat until crisp and toasted, 3–4 minutes. Set aside to cool.
2. Combine the salad greens, blueberries, cheese, and parsley in a salad bowl.

Vinaigrette

1. Whisk the oil, vinegar, garlic, salt, and pepper in a small bowl.
2. Pour over the salad and toss gently to coat. Sprinkle with the walnuts, and serve.

If you liked this recipe, you will love these as well.

AVOCADO & SPINACH
salad

HALLOUMI & MELON
salad

BLUE CHEESE
& STRAWBERRY salad

Farro is an old-fashioned Italian wheat. If you can't find it for this recipe, replace with the same quantity of spelt or pearl barley.

FARRO TABBOULEH with boiled eggs

2	cups (400 g) farro
2	cups (200 g) chopped fresh flat-leaf parsley
$^1/_4$	cup chopped fresh mint
$^1/_2$	cup chopped fresh cilantro (coriander)
20	cherry tomatoes, halved or quartered, depending on size
6	scallions (spring onions), finely chopped
1	teaspoon ground sumac
$^1/_3$	cup (90 ml) freshly squeezed lemon juice
	Freshly ground sea salt and black pepper
$^1/_4$	cup (60 ml) extra-virgin olive oil
6	large eggs

Serves 6 • Preparation 15 minutes + 2–3 hours to chill • Cooking 40 minutes • Difficulty 1

1. Cook the farro in a pot of lightly salted boiling water until tender, about 40 minutes, or for the time indicated on the package. Drain well, and set aside to cool.

2. Combine the parsley, mint, cilantro, tomatoes, scallions, farro, sumac, and lemon juice in a large bowl. Season with salt and pepper, tossing gently to mix.

3. Cover the bowl with a clean cloth or plastic wrap (cling film) and chill for 2–3 hours.

4. Boil the eggs until firm but not hard, 6–8 minutes. Peel and cut into quarters lengthwise.

5. Add the cherry tomatoes and oil to the farro mixture, tossing gently to combine. Divide the salad among six serving bowls, top with the eggs, and serve.

If you liked this recipe, you will love these as well.

BLACK LENTIL salad

QUINOA SALAD with zucchini & feta cheese

GRILLED ZUCCHINI SALAD with goat cheese

SPINACH & CHEESE salad

Serves 4 • Preparation 15 minutes • Difficulty 1

7	cups (350 g) baby spinach leaves		cheese, in flakes
2	carrots, peeled lengthwise into thin julienne strips	1/2	teaspoon sea salt flakes Freshly squeezed juice of 1 lemon
1	cup (150 g) canned corn kernels, or 8 baby corn cobs	1/4	cup (60 ml) extra-virgin olive oil Freshly ground black pepper
1 1/4	cups (120 g) Parmesan		

1. Trim the stems and discard any bruised spinach leaves, wash thoroughly, drain and dry on a clean kitchen towel. Shred the carrots into julienne strips.

2. Place the spinach in a large round dish or low, wide salad bowl and sprinkle with the carrots and corn. Top with the flakes of cheese.

3. Dissolve the salt in the lemon juice in small bowl. Add the oil and pepper, and whisk to blend.

4. Dress the salad 5 minutes before serving.

BLACK LENTIL salad

Serves 4 • Preparation 10 minutes • Cooking 15–20 minutes Difficulty 1

1 1/2	cups (350 g) black beluga lentils	8	ounces (250 g) feta cheese, crumbled
3	tablespoons extra-virgin olive oil Freshly squeezed juice of 1 lemon	24	cherry tomatoes, halved
		1	red onion, sliced Fresh cilantro (coriander) leaves
1	clove garlic, minced		

1. Put the lentils in a medium saucepan and cover with plenty of cold water. Bring to a boil over high heat, then gently simmer until tender, 15–20 minutes.

2. Drain the lentils and transfer to a medium bowl. Drizzle with the oil, lemon juice, and garlic while still warm. Toss gently.

3. Let cool to room temperature, then pile into a large salad bowl. Add the feta, cherry tomatoes, and onion and toss gently. Garnish with the cilantro and serve.

AVOCADO & SPINACH salad

Serves 4 • Preparation 15 minutes • Difficulty 1

2	large ripe oranges	2	scallions (spring onions), trimmed and sliced
5	cups (250 g) baby spinach leaves		Finely grated zest of 1 orange
2	large ripe avocados, peeled, pitted, and sliced Freshly squeezed juice of 1 lemon		Freshly ground sea salt and black pepper
1/4	cup (60 ml) extra-virgin olive oil		

1. Peel the oranges using a sharp knife, removing all the bitter white pith. Break the fruit into segments.

2. Put the spinach leaves in a large salad bowl. Top with the oranges and avocados.

3. Beat the lemon juice and oil in a small bowl with a fork. Add the scallions and orange zest and season with salt and pepper. Beat well.

4. Drizzle the dressing over the salad, toss carefully, and serve.

HALLOUMI & MELON salad

Serves 4 • Preparation 10 minutes + 10–15 minutes to cool Cooking 5 minutes • Difficulty 1

1	small watermelon, weighing about 2 pounds (1 kg)	8	ounces (250 g) halloumi cheese, sliced Finely grated zest and freshly squeezed juice of 1 unwaxed lemon
1	small bunch fresh cilantro (coriander) leaves	1/4	cup (60 ml) extra-virgin olive oil
1	small bunch fresh parsley leaves		

1. Peel the watermelon and remove the seeds. Slice into small cubes or triangles and place in a large salad bowl. Add the cilantro and parsley.

2. Heat a grill pan (griddle pan) until very hot and grill the cheese until browned on both sides, about 5 minutes. Let cool for 10–15 minutes before adding to the salad bowl.

3. Whisk the lemon juice and zest with the oil in a small bowl. Drizzle over the salad, toss gently, and serve.

Avocados are packed with nutrients that help to prevent inflammation in the body and they also contain compounds that help you to absorb antioxidants from other healthy ingredients in your salads.

AVOCADO, FAVA & FETA salad

3	cups (450 g) frozen fava beans (broad beans)
2	avocados, pitted, peeled, and chopped
1/4	cup fresh chopped cilantro (coriander)
1/4	cup fresh chopped basil
1/4	cup fresh chopped parsley
4	scallions (spring onions), thinly sliced
5	ounces (150 g) feta cheese, crumbled or cubed
16	cherry tomatoes, halved
1	sweet red onion, thinly sliced
	Freshly squeezed juice of 1 lime
	Freshly ground sea salt and black pepper
1/4	cup (60 ml) extra-virgin olive oil

Serves 4-6 • Preparation 15 minutes + 10 minutes to cool • Cooking 5 minutes • Difficulty 1

1. Cook the fava beans in lightly salted boiling water until just tender, about 5 minutes. Drain and set aside to cool for 10 minutes.

2. Combine the fava beans, avocado, cilantro, basil, parsley, scallions, feta, tomatoes, onion, and lime juice in a large salad bowl.

3. Season with salt and pepper and drizzle with the oil. Toss gently, and serve.

If you liked this recipe, you will love these as well.

CHEESE, WALNUT & BLUEBERRY salad

FAVA BEAN FATTOUSH with feta cheese

WARM SPRING VEGETABLE salad

ROASTED BUTTERNUT & LENTIL salad

Salad

4	pounds (2 kg) butternut squash, peeled and cut into 1-inch (2.5-cm) cubes
2	tablespoons extra-virgin olive oil
	Freshly ground sea salt and black pepper
1½	cups (280 g) green Le Puy lentils
2	cups (100 g) arugula (rocket)
1	tablespoon sesame seeds, toasted
6	scallions (spring onions), thinly sliced

Dressing

5	tablespoons (75 ml) extra-virgin olive oil
3	tablespoons balsamic vinegar
1	tablespoon soy sauce
1	red chili, seeded and finely chopped
1	clove garlic, finely chopped
1	teaspoon clear honey

Serves 6 • Preparation 20 minutes • Cooking 30–40 minutes • Difficulty 1

Salad

1. Preheat the oven to 400°F (200°C/gas 6). Put the squash in a roasting pan, drizzle with 1 tablespoon of oil, and season with salt and pepper. Roast for about 30 minutes, until tender.

2. Cook the lentils in a pot of lightly salted boiling water until tender but not mushy, 20–25 minutes. Remove from the heat, drain, and set aside to cool a little.

Dressing

1. Whisk the oil, balsamic vinegar, soy sauce, chili, garlic, and honey in a small bowl.

2. Put the arugula in a shallow serving bowl and top with the lentils and squash. Drizzle with the dressing, sprinkle with the sesame seeds and scallions, and serve.

ROASTED VEGGIES with garbanzos

1 large red onion, cut into wedges

2 zucchini (courgettes), thickly sliced

2 red bell peppers (capsicums), seeded and cut into large chunks

1 pound (500 g) vine tomatoes

Freshly ground sea salt and black pepper

6 tablespoons (90 ml) extra-virgin olive oil

Freshly squeezed juice of $1/2$ lemon

2 tablespoons finely chopped fresh parsley

2 (14-ounce/400-g) cans garbanzo beans (chickpeas), drained and rinsed

5 ounces (150 g) feta cheese, crumbled

Serves 4 • Preparation 15 minutes • Cooking 30 minutes • Difficulty 1

1. Preheat the oven to 425°F (220°C/gas 7).

2. Put the onion, zucchini, bell peppers, and tomatoes in a large shallow roasting pan and season with salt and pepper. Drizzle with 4 tablespoons of oil and toss well. Roast for 30 minutes, stirring halfway through, until the vegetables are tender and beginning to brown.

3. Whisk the lemon juice and the remaining 2 tablespoons of oil in a small bowl. Season with salt and pepper and stir in the parsley.

4. When the vegetables are cooked, let cool for 5 minutes, then transfer to a bowl with the garbanzo beans and feta. Drizzle with the dressing, toss gently, and serve.

Serve this tasty salad for lunch. If you don't like spicy food, leave the chili out.

QUINOA SALAD with zucchini & feta cheese

Salad

$1^1/_2$	cups (300 g) quinoa
2	zucchini (courgettes)
6	scallions (spring onions), thinly sliced
24	cherry tomatoes, halved
1	red chili, seeded and finely chopped
7	ounces (200 g) feta cheese, crumbled
	Small bunch fresh parsley, coarsely chopped

Dressing

$1/_3$	cup (90 ml) extra-virgin olive oil
2	tablespoons balsamic vinegar
	Freshly ground sea salt and black pepper

Serves 4 • Preparation 15 minutes • Cooking 15 minutes • Difficulty 1

Salad

1. Rinse the quinoa under cold running water. This will remove any traces of the bitter saponin that covers these grains.

2. Put the quinoa in a saucepan with 6 cups (1.5 liters) of water. Bring to a boil, then simmer until tender, about 15 minutes. Drain well and set aside to cool.

3. Cut the ends off the zucchini, then cut lengthwise into long thin ribbons using a potato peeler.

Dressing

1. Whisk the oil and vinegar in a small bowl. Season with salt and pepper.

2. Combine the quinoa, zucchini, scallions, cherry tomatoes, chili, feta, and parsley in a large bowl. Drizzle with the dressing, toss gently, and serve.

If you liked this recipe, you will love these as well.

QUINOA SALAD
with corn & beans

QUINOA SALAD
with grapefruit

QUINOA SALAD
with feta & almonds

GRILLED ZUCCHINI SALAD with goat cheese

3	large zucchini (courgettes), sliced into thin strips lengthwise
5	tablespoons (75 ml) extra-virgin olive oil
1	tablespoon fennel seeds
5	ounces (150 g) sliced bacon, rinds removed and chopped
1	large fennel bulb, thinly sliced
8	ounces (250 g) soft goat cheese, crumbled
	Freshly squeezed juice of 1 small lemon
	Freshly ground sea salt and black pepper
	Fresh parsley, to garnish

Serves 4 • Preparation 15 minutes + 10 minutes to rest • Cooking 10–15 minutes • Difficulty 1

1. Toss the zucchini in a bowl with 2 tablespoons of oil and the fennel seeds and leave for 10 minutes.

2. Heat a grill pan (griddle) over medium-high heat and grill the zucchini for a few minutes on each side until tender.

3. Dry-fry the bacon in a large frying pan until crisp, about 5 minutes, then drain on kitchen paper.

4. Place the fennel in a large bowl and mix with the warm zucchini, bacon, and goat cheese.

5. Whisk the lemon juice with the remaining 3 tablespoons of oil. Season with salt and pepper and drizzle over the salad. Garnish with the parsley, and serve.

COLESLAW with roasted peanuts

4 cups (200 g) finely shredded white cabbage

1 large carrot, coarsely grated

1/3 cup (60 g) golden raisins (sultanas)

4 scallions (spring onions), finely chopped, white and green parts separate

2 tablespoons mayonnaise

2/3 cup (150 g) plain yogurt

1 teaspoon Dijon mustard

1 tablespoon mango chutney

Freshly ground black pepper

6 radishes, thinly sliced

1/2 cup (90 g) salted, roasted peanuts

2 tablespoons finely chopped fresh parsley

2 tablespoons snipped fresh chives

Serves 4–6 • Preparation 15 minutes • Cooking 15–20 minutes
Difficulty 1

1. Mix the cabbage, carrot, golden raisins, and the white parts of the scallions in a large bowl.

2. Stir the mayonnaise, yogurt, mustard, and mango chutney in a bowl and season with pepper. Stir into the cabbage mixture, tossing well to coat.

3. Just before serving, stir in the radishes and peanuts and sprinkle with the chopped green parts of the scallions, the parsley, and chives.

The small, dark green lentils from Le Puy in France are easily the best type of lentil for salads. Not only do they have a delicious flavor, but they hold their shape well during cooking, and add a wonderful greeny-brown color to the finished dish.

LENTIL & HALLOUMI salad

1½	cups (280 g) green Le Puy lentils
	Sea salt
8	ounces (250 g) halloumi cheese, sliced about ½-inch (1-cm) thick
24	cherry tomatoes, halved
1	small red onion, finely chopped
1	clove garlic, finely chopped
3	tablespoons freshly squeezed lemon juice
5	tablespoons (75) extra-virgin olive oil
	Freshly ground black pepper
	Small bunch fresh cilantro (coriander), coarsely chopped

Serves 4–6 • Preparation 20 minutes • Cooking 25–30 minutes
Difficulty 2

1. Put the lentils and ½ teaspoon of salt in a medium pot and cover with 6 cups (1.5 liters) of cold water. Bring to a boil, then simmer over low heat until the lentils are tender but not mushy, about 25 minutes.

2. Remove from the heat, drain, and set aside to cool a little.

3. Heat a grill pan (griddle) or large frying pan over medium-high heat. Brush the halloumi on both sides with 1 tablespoon of the oil. Add the halloumi to the hot pan and cook until golden brown, 1–2 minutes each side.

4. Combine the cherry tomatoes, onion, garlic, lemon juice, and remaining oil in a bowl. Add the lentils and toss gently. Season with pepper.

5. Add the cheese and cilantro, stir gently, and serve.

If you liked this recipe, you will love these as well.

GRILLED HALLOUMI
with oranges, watercress & mint

BLACK LENTIL
salad

BEAN SALAD
with tuna, eggs & olives

FAVA BEAN FATTOUSH with feta cheese

3	whole-wheat (wholemeal) pita breads
1	pound (500 g) fresh or frozen fava (broad) beans
1	cucumber
	Finely grated zest and juice of 1 unwaxed lemon
1/2	cup (120 ml) extra-virgin olive oil
1	teaspoon sugar
	Freshly ground sea salt and black pepper
1/2	cup coarsely chopped fresh mint
1/2	cup coarsely chopped fresh parsley
	Small bunch fresh chives, snipped
8	ounces (250 g) feta cheese, crumbled

Serves 4–6 • Preparation 30 minutes • Cooking 10–15 minutes
Difficulty 1

1. Preheat the oven to 350°F (180°C/gas 4). Spread the pita bread out on a large baking sheet. Bake until crisp and golden brown, 5–10 minutes. Set aside to cool.

2. Bring a pan of lightly salted water to a boil. Add the fava beans and simmer until just tender, 3–4 minutes. Drain and set aside until cool enough to handle. Transfer to a bowl.

3. Halve the cucumber lengthwise, scrape out the seeds with a teaspoon, then slice thinly and add to the beans.

4. Whisk the lemon zest, juice, oil, sugar, salt, and pepper is a small bowl. Drizzle over the beans and cucumber. Add the mint and parsley and toss well.

5. Tear the toasted pita into pieces and add to the salad with the crumbled feta. Toss gently, and serve.

BEAN SALAD with tuna, eggs & olives

Salad

2	large eggs
2	(14-ounce/400-g) cans white kidney beans, drained and rinsed
1	(12-ounce/350-g) can tuna, drained
1/2	cup (50 g) large black olives

Dressing

1/4	cup (60 ml) extra-virgin olive oil
2	tablespoons balsamic vinegar
1	tablespoon finely chopped fresh mint
1	tablespoon finely chopped fresh marjoram
2	tablespoons finely chopped fresh parsley + extra sprigs, to garnish
	Sea salt flakes

Serves 4 • Preparation 10 minutes • Cooking 7 minutes • Difficulty 1

Salad

1. Bring the eggs to a boil in a small saucepan of water and boil for 7 minutes. Drain and rinse under cold running water. Shell the eggs and cut into wedges.

Dressing

1. Whisk the oil, vinegar, mint, marjoram, and parsley in a small bowl. Season with salt.

2. Put the beans in a large salad bowl and add the tuna and olives. Drizzle with the dressing and toss well. Add the eggs. Garnish with the sprigs of parsley, and serve.

Beans are high in protein, complex carbohydrates, folate, and iron. They are packed with fiber and antioxidants that are believed to help prevent cancer, lower cholesterol, prevent weight gain, and help manage blood sugar levels.

SPICY BEAN salad

Salad

4	large eggs
2	avocados, peeled and stoned
2	(14-ounce/400-g) cans red kidney beans
1	red onion, thinly sliced
	Large bunch fresh cilantro (coriander), leaves only, coarsely chopped
25	cherry tomatoes, halved
	Toasted tortillas, to serve

Dressing

1/3	cup (90 ml) extra-virgin olive oil
2	tablespoons balsamic vinegar
1	red chili, seeded and thinly sliced
1	teaspoon ground cumin
	Freshly ground sea salt and black pepper

Serves 4–6 • Preparation 15 minutes • Cooking 7–8 minutes • Difficulty 1

Salad

1. Lower the eggs into boiling water and simmer for 7–8 minutes. Place in a bowl of cold water to cool.

2. Slice the avocados and place in a large bowl with the beans, onion, cilantro, and cherry tomatoes.

Dressing

1. Whisk the oil, vinegar, chili, cumin, salt, and pepper in a small bowl.

2. When the eggs are cool enough to handle, peel and cut in half. Add to the salad in the bowl.

3. Drizzle with the dressing. Toss gently and serve with the tortillas.

If you liked this recipe, you will love these as well.

LENTIL & HALLOUMI salad

BEAN SALAD with bell pepper & onion

BLACK BEAN, AVOCADO & EGG salad

CANNELLINI SALAD with roasted tomatoes

24	cherry or vine tomatoes, halved
4	tablespoons (60 ml) extra-virgin olive oil
	Freshly ground sea salt and black pepper
5	ounces (150 g) chorizo, sliced and quartered
1	red onion, finely chopped
2	tablespoons sherry vinegar
2	tablespoons honey
2	(14-ounce/400-g) cans cannellini beans, drained and rinsed
2	cups (100 g) arugula (rocket)

Serves 4–6 • Preparation 15 minutes • Cooking 25–30 minutes
Difficulty 1

1. Preheat the oven to 350°F (180°C/gas 4). Put the tomatoes on a large baking sheet and drizzle with 2 tablespoons of the oil. Season with salt and pepper and roast for 20 minutes, until softened and almost collapsing.

2. While the tomatoes are roasting, dry-fry the chorizo in a large frying pan over medium heat until crisp, 3–4 minutes. Drain on paper towels.

3. Return the pan to medium heat and add the remaining 2 tablespoons of oil and the onion. season with salt and pepper. Sauté until the onion is softened, 3–4 minutes. Stir in the vinegar and simmer until reduced by half. Add the honey and stir well.

4. Put the beans in a large salad bowl. Pour the warm onion mixture over the top, tossing gently. Add the chorizo, cherry tomatoes, and arugula, toss again, and serve.

BEAN SALAD with bell pepper & onion

Salad

1 (14-ounce/400-g) can
  cranberry or borlotti beans,
  drained and rinsed

1 (14-ounce/400-g) can
  cannellini or white kidney
  beans, drained and rinsed

1 large red bell pepper
  (capsicum), seeded and finely
  sliced

1 sweet red onion, thinly sliced

1 clove garlic, finely chopped

4 tablespoons finely chopped
  fresh parsley + extra leaves,
  to garnish

3 cups (150 g) mixed baby salad
  greens

Dressing

$\frac{1}{4}$ cup (60 ml) extra-virgin olive
  oil

  Freshly squeezed juice of
  1 lemon

  Freshly ground sea salt and
  black pepper

Serves 4–6 • Preparation 15 minutes + 30 minutes to rest • Cooking 15–20 minutes • Difficulty 1

Salad

1. Place both types of bean in a large bowl. Add the bell pepper, onion, garlic, and parsley and toss well to mix.

Dressing

1. Whisk the oil and lemon juice in a small bowl with a fork. Season with salt and pepper. Drizzle the dressing over the salad. Toss well, cover, and let rest for 30 minutes.

2. Arrange the salad greens in a large salad bowl. Spoon the bean salad over the top. Garnish with the sprigs of parsley and serve.

Serve this salad in the springtime when new potatoes, fava beans, and asparagus return to the markets after the long winter.

WARM SPRING VEGETABLE salad

Salad

1	pound (500 g) new potatoes, halved if large
1	cup (150 g) baby fava (broad) beans
1	bunch fresh very tender asparagus
1	cup (150 g) fresh baby peas
3$^1/_2$	ounces (100 g) prosciutto, thinly sliced
3	cups (150 g) mixed salad leaves
3$^1/_2$	ounces (100 g) Parmesan cheese, shaved

Dressing

2	ounces (60 g) freshly grated Parmesan cheese
1	cup (50 g) watercress
$^1/_3$	cup (90 ml) extra-virgin olive oil
2	tablespoons cider vinegar
	Pinch of sugar
	Freshly ground sea salt and black pepper

Serves 4 • Preparation 15 minutes • Cooking 15–20 minutes
Difficulty 1

Salad

1. Cook the potatoes in lightly salted boiling water until tender, 10–15 minutes. Drain and set aside. Blanch the fava beans and asparagus in boiling salted water until just tender, 2–3 minutes. Drain and let cool in a colander. Blanch the peas in a separate pan for 1 minute. Drain well.

2. Toss the asparagus, beans, peas, potatoes, and prosciutto together in a salad bowl.

Dressing

1. Put the cheese, watercress, oil, cider vinegar, and sugar in a food processor and chop until smooth. Season with salt and pepper.

2. Toss the salad leaves with half the dressing and arrange on four serving plates. Pile the vegetable mixture on top and drizzle with the remaining dressing. Top with the cheese shavings, and serve.

If you liked this recipe, you will love these as well.

POTATO SALAD
with bacon & blue cheese

POTATO SALAD
with cherry tomatoes & olives

WATERMELON SALAD
with prosciutto & feta

LENTIL & FENNEL SALAD with walnut dressing

Salad

1	cup (150 g) green Le Puy lentils
1	bay leaf
1	shallot, peeled
1	large or 2 small fennel bulbs, thinly sliced tip to base
2	cups (100 g) watercress
1	crisp eating apple (such as Cox), cored and thinly sliced

Dressing

$1/2$	cup (60 g) walnuts, coarsely chopped
	Pinch of sea salt flakes
$1/8$	teaspoon hot smoked paprika
1	teaspoon walnut oil
2	teaspoons Dijon mustard
1	clove garlic, finely chopped
3	tablespoons red wine vinegar
$1/2$	cup (120 ml) extra-virgin olive oil
	Pinch of sugar

Serves 4 • Preparation 15 minutes • Cooking 25 minutes • Difficulty 1

Salad

1. Put the lentils, bay leaf, shallot, and 1/2 teaspoon of salt in a medium pot and cover with 6 cups (1.5 liters) of cold water. Bring to a boil, then simmer over low heat until the lentils are tender but not mushy, about 25 minutes.

Dressing

1. Mix the walnuts in a frying pan with the salt, paprika, and walnut oil, and fry over low heat for 2–3 minutes, shaking the pan to move the nuts about. Set aside to cool.

2. Put all the remaining dressing ingredients into a screw-top jar and shake until blended. Add the walnut mixture to the dressing in the jar.

3. Drain the lentils, discarding the shallot and bay leaf. Stir two-thirds of the dressing into the warm lentils. Let cool.

4. Pile two-thirds of the lentils into serving plates. Top with fennel, watercress, and apple mixture. Top with the remaining lentils, drizzle with the remaining dressing, and serve.

BLACK BEAN, AVOCADO & EGG salad

Salad

2	avocados, peeled and pitted
1	(14-ounce/400-g) can black beans, drained and rinsed
1	(14-ounce/400-g) can white kidney beans, drained and rinsed
1	small red onion, finely sliced
1	cup (50 g) coarsely chopped fresh cilantro (coriander)
24	cherry tomatoes, halved
4	hard-boiled eggs
	Toasted pita bread, to serve

Dressing

$1/3$	cup (90 ml) extra-virgin olive oil
1	tablespoon freshly squeezed lime juice
1	clove garlic, minced
$1/4$	teaspoon sea salt flakes
	Freshly ground black pepper
	Pinch of sugar
1	small red chili, seeded and finely chopped
$1/2$	teaspoon ground cumin

Serves 4–6 • Preparation 10 minutes • Difficulty 1

Salad

1. Slice the avocados and place in a large bowl with both types of beans, the onion, cilantro, and tomatoes.

Dressing

1. Whisk the oil, lime juice, garlic, salt, pepper, sugar, chili, and cumin in a small bowl.
2. Shell the eggs and cut into quarters.
3. Toss the salad with the dressing and top with the eggs. Serve with the pita bread.

Serve small bowls of this delicious salad as an appetizer before a more substantial course, or pile it into plates and serve as a one-dish lunch. This recipe will serve six as an appetizer and two to four as a one-dish meal.

BLUE CHEESE & STRAWBERRY salad

Serves 4 • Preparation 15 minutes • Cooking 5 minutes • Difficulty 1

Dressing

1/2   cup (120 ml) extra-virgin olive oil

1/4   cup (60 ml) balsamic vinegar

1   teaspoon Dijon mustard

     Salt and freshly ground black pepper

Salad

4   large slices firm-textured bread

1–2   cloves garlic

3   cups (150 g) arugula (rocket)

2   cups (300 g) strawberries, halved

4   large thin slices prosciutto, torn

8   ounces (250 g) blue cheese, crumbled

Dressing

1. Whisk the oil, balsamic vinegar, and mustard in a small bowl. Season with salt and pepper, whisking to combine.

Salad

1. Preheat the oven to 400°F (200°C/gas 6). Toast the bread in the oven until crisp and golden brown, about 5 minutes. Let cool a little, then run all over with the garlic. Tear into pieces.

2. Combine the arugula and strawberries in a large bowl. Add the prosciutto, bread, and crumbled blue cheese. Toss gently to combine.

3. Drizzle with the dressing, toss gently, and serve immediately.

If you liked this recipe, you will love these as well.

73
CHEESE, WALNUT & BLUEBERRY salad

76
AVOCADO & SPINACH salad

85
COLESLAW with roasted peanuts

WATERMELON SALAD with prosciutto & feta

Salad

$1/2$	small watermelon, peeled, seeds removed, and cut in small cubes
8	ounces (250 g) feta cheese, cut into small cubes
2	cups (100 g) baby arugula (rocket) leaves
8	large thin slices prosciutto, cut in quarters

Vinaigrette

2	tablespoons freshly squeezed lime juice
$1/3$	cup (90 ml) extra-virgin olive oil
1	teaspoon Dijon mustard
	Freshly ground sea salt and black pepper

Serves 4 • Preparation 15 minutes • Difficulty 1

Salad

1. Combine the watermelon, feta, and arugula in a large shallow serving platter. Toss gently. Top with the prosciutto.

Vinaigrette

1. Whisk the lime juice, oil, and mustard in a small bowl. Season with salt and pepper.

2. Drizzle over the salad, and serve.

MEDITERRANEAN salad

Salad

8	ounces (250 g) firm cheese, such as feta or Fontina, cut into small cubes
20	cherry tomatoes, halved
2	cucumbers, peeled
1	cup (100 g) small black olives
1	medium red onion, sliced
	Handful fresh mint leaves

Dressing

½	cup (120 ml) extra-virgin olive oil
	Freshly squeezed juice of 1 lemon
1	teaspoon Dijon mustard
	Freshly ground sea salt and black pepper

Serves 4–6 • Preparation 15 minutes • Difficulty 1

Salad

1. Combine the cheese, cherry tomatoes, and cucumbers in a large salad bowl. Add the olives, onion, and mint.

Dressing

1. Whisk the oil, lemon juice, mustard, salt, and pepper in a small bowl until well mixed.

2. Drizzle the salad with the dressing, toss well, and serve.

classic salads

NIÇOISE salad

Salad

8	medium firm tomatoes, each cut into 8 wedges
	Sea salt flakes
3	cups (150 g) mixed salad greens
1	red bell pepper (capsicum), seeded and cut into thin strips
8	ounces (250 g) canned tuna, drained
3	stalks celery, thinly sliced
3	shallots, finely chopped
12	black olives
6	salt-cured anchovy fillets
4	hard-boiled eggs, quartered

Vinaigrette

1/2	cup (120 ml) extra-virgin olive oil
2	tablespoons white wine vinegar
1	teaspoon Dijon mustard
	Freshly ground sea salt and black pepper

Serves 4 • Preparation 15 minutes + 1 hour to drain • Difficulty 1

Salad

1. Place the tomatoes in a colander and sprinkle lightly with salt. Let stand for 1 hour to drain.

2. Arrange the salad greens in four salad bowls with the tomatoes. Top the bell pepper, tuna, celery, and shallots. Arrange the olives and anchovy fillets on top. Garnish with the boiled eggs.

Vinaigrette

1. Whisk the oil, vinegar, mustard, salt, and pepper in a small bowl.

2. Drizzle the vinaigrette over the salad, and serve.

If you liked this recipe, you will love these as well.

GREEK salad

CAPRESE salad

COBB salad

This is the classic version of this wonderful salad. There are many variations: try adding a teaspoon of finely chopped lemon zest (yellow part only), or some fresh basil leaves.

GREEK salad

8	large vine tomatoes, cut into wedges
2	cucumbers, peeled, seeded, then coarsely chopped
1	red onion, halved and thinly sliced
30	Kalamata olives
7	ounces (200 g) feta cheese, cut into chunks
1–2	teaspoons dried oregano
	Freshly ground sea salt and black pepper
1/2	cup (120 ml) extra-virgin olive oil
	Pita bread, to serve

Serves 6 • Preparation 15 minutes • Difficulty 1

1. Combine the tomatoes, cucumbers, onion, olives, and feta in a large bowl.

2. Dust with the oregano and season with salt and pepper. Drizzle with the oil and toss gently.

3. Serve with the pita bread.

If you liked this recipe, you will love these as well.

LENTIL & HALLOUMI
salad

MEDITERRANEAN
salad

CAPRESE salad

PANZANELLA
(Tuscan bread salad)

4–6 thick slices day-old firm-textured bread

4–5 tablespoons cold water

6 firm-ripe vine tomatoes, chopped

1 small red onion, thinly sliced

1 small cucumber, peeled and cut into small cubes

1 tablespoon brine-cured capers, drained

½ cup fresh basil leaves

  Freshly ground sea salt and black pepper

⅓ cup (90 ml) extra-virgin olive oil

2 tablespoons red wine vinegar

Serves 4–6 • Preparation 15 minutes + 30 minutes to rest • Difficulty 1

1. Tear the bread into bite-size chunks. Place in a bowl and drizzle with the water. Mix well, so that the bread begins to break down a little. Squeeze out any excess moisture.

2. Add the tomatoes, onion, cucumber, capers, and basil. Mix well, then set aside to rest for 30 minutes.

3. Season with salt and pepper. Drizzle with the oil and vinegar and mix well again before serving.

CAPRESE salad

4–6 medium red vine tomatoes
1 pound (500 g) very fresh mozzarella di buffalo cheese
20 large basil leaves
Freshly ground sea salt and black pepper
$^{1}/_{2}$ cup (90 ml) extra-virgin olive oil
$^{1}/_{2}$ teaspoon dried oregano (optional)
Freshly baked bread, to serve

Serves 4–6 • Preparation 10 minutes • Difficulty 1

1. Cut the tomatoes in $^{1}/_{4}$-inch (6-mm) thick slices and arrange on a flat serving dish.

2. Cut the mozzarella in slices of the same width and alternate with the tomato. Sprinkle with basil, salt, and pepper, and drizzle with the oil. Sprinkle with the oregano, if using.

3. Serve with the bread to mop up the oil and tomato juices.

COLESLAW

Serves 4 • Preparation 15 minutes + 2 hours to chill
Difficulty 1

Salad

1	medium head cabbage (about 4–5 cups), shredded	1	apple, peeled, cored and coarsely grated
1	medium green bell pepper (capsicum), thinly sliced	2	tablespoons freshly squeezed lemon juice
3	carrots, coarsely shredded		**Dressing**
1	small onion, grated	3/4	cup (180 ml) mayonnaise
2–3	tablespoons golden raisins	2	tablespoons sugar
		1/2	teaspoon sea salt
		1/4	cup (60 ml) vinegar
		2	tablespoons extra-virgin olive oil

Salad

1. Combine all the salad ingredients in a large bowl. Cover and chill for at least 2 hours.

Dressing

1. Whisk the mayonnaise, sugar, salt, vinegar, and oil in a small bowl until smooth.

2. Pour over the coleslaw in the bowl, toss, and serve.

BLT salad

Serves 4 • Preparation 15 minutes • Cooking 10–15 minutes
Difficulty 1

Salad

2	cups (120 g) cubed bread		**Dressing**
8	slices bacon, rinds removed	1	large tomato, halved
3	tomatoes, sliced	1/3	cup (90 ml) mayonnaise
5	cups (250 g) chopped romaine (cos) lettuce	2	tablespoons finely chopped fresh chives
		1	tablespoon white wine vinegar
		1	clove garlic, minced Freshly ground black pepper

Salad

1. Preheat the oven to 400°F (200°C/gas 6). Bake the bread until golden brown, 10 minutes. Set aside.

2. Dry-fry the bacon in a large frying pan over medium heat until crisp, about 5 minutes. Drain on paper towels. Let cool, then crumble and set aside.

Dressing

1. Working over a bowl, shred both halves of the tomato on the large holes of a grater. Discard the skin. Add the mayonnaise, chives, vinegar, garlic, and pepper and whisk to combine.

2. Combine the tomatoes, lettuce, bread, and bacon in a bowl. Drizzle with the dressing, toss, and serve.

TUNA & BEAN salad

Serves 2–4 • Preparation 15 minutes • Difficulty 1

Salad

1	(8-ounce/250-g) can tuna, drained		**Dressing**
1	(14-ounce/400-g) can butter beans, drained	1/4	cup (60 ml) extra-virgin olive oil
1	small red onion, thinly sliced		Freshly squeezed juice of 1/2 lemon
24	cherry tomatoes, halved	1	teaspoon Dijon mustard Salt and freshly ground black pepper
1/2	cup (25 g) fresh basil leaves		

Salad

1. Flake the tuna with a fork and place in a salad bowl. Add the butter beans, onion, cherry tomatoes, and basil and toss gently.

Dressing

1. Whisk the oil, lemon juice, and mustard together in a small bowl. Season with salt and pepper.

2. Drizzle over the salad, toss gently, and serve.

TABBOULEH

Serves 4 • Preparation 15 minutes + 1 hour to rest
Difficulty 1

1	cup (150 g) fine bulgur Freshly ground sea salt and black pepper	2	medium-large tomatoes, cut into small cubes
1/2	cup finely chopped fresh mint	3/4	cup (180 ml) extra-virgin olive oil
1 1/2	cups (75 g) finely chopped fresh parsley	1	cup (250 ml) freshly squeezed lemon juice
1	small red onion, finely chopped		

1. Combine the bulgur and 2–3 pinches of salt in a medium bowl and pour in 3 cups (750 ml) of boiling water. Stir gently, cover with a clean cloth, and let stand until tender, about 30 minutes.

2. Squeeze out any excess moisture from the bulgur and transfer to a salad bowl. Add the mint, parsley, onion, and tomatoes, and toss well.

3. Drizzle with the oil and lemon juice. Season with salt and pepper and toss again.

4. Let rest for at least 30 minutes before serving.

INDONESIAN CHICKEN salad

Salad

2	boneless skinless chicken breasts
	Freshly ground sea salt and black pepper
14	ounces (400 g) new potatoes
3	scallions (spring onions), thinly sliced
1	large carrot, coarsely grated
½	cucumber, with peel, cut into matchsticks
1	small pineapple, peeled, cored, and diced
1	cup (50 g) bean sprouts
½	cup (60 g) unsalted peanuts
	Fresh cilantro (coriander) leaves to garnish

Dressing

½	cup (120 g) peanut butter
2	tablespoons soy sauce
1	small red chili, finely chopped
1	teaspoon finely grated ginger
5	tablespoons (75 ml) sesame oil
	Freshly squeezed juice of 1 lime

Serves 4 • Preparation 15 minutes • Cooking 20–30 minutes • Difficulty 1

Salad

1. Tenderize the chicken breasts gently with a steak hammer. Season with salt and pepper. Preheat a grill pan (griddle) and grill over low heat until cooked through, 10–15 minutes. Let cool a little, then cut into small pieces.

2. Cook the potatoes in a pan of lightly salted boiling water until tender, 10–15 minutes. Drain and set aside.

3. Combine the chicken, potatoes, scallions, carrot, cucumber, pineapple, bean sprouts, and peanuts in a large salad bowl.

Dressing

1. Put the peanut butter in a small bowl and add the soy sauce, chili, ginger, oil, and lime juice, stirring until smooth.

2. Pour the dressing over the salad. Garnish with the cilantro, and serve.

CHICKEN CAESAR salad

Salad

4	thick slices crusty white bread, torn into pieces
3	tablespoons extra-virgin olive oil
	Freshly ground sea salt and black pepper
2	boneless skinless chicken breasts
6	slices bacon, rinds removed
1	large romaine (cos) lettuce, leaves separated
3	ounces (90 g) Parmesan cheese, in shavings

Dressing

4	anchovy fillets
1/2	cup (120 ml) mayonnaise
1	clove garlic, finely chopped
2	tablespoons finely grated Parmesan cheese
1	tablespoon white wine vinegar

Serves 4 • Preparation 15 minutes • Cooking 15–25 minutes • Difficulty 1

Salad

1. Preheat the oven to 400°F (200°C/gas 6). Spread the bread out on a baking sheet and drizzle with 2 tablespoons of oil. Season with salt and pepper. Bake for 8–10 minutes, until golden brown.

2. Rub the chicken with the remaining 1 tablespoon of oil. Season with salt and pepper. Heat a grill pan (griddle) over medium heat. Grill the chicken until tender, 4–6 minutes each side. Coarsely chop or tear into pieces.

3. Dry-fry the bacon in a large frying pan over medium heat until crisp and golden brown, about 5 minutes.

Dressing

1. Mash the anchovies with a fork in a small bowl. Stir in the mayonnaise, garlic, Parmesan, and vinegar.

2. Toss the lettuce, chicken, bread, bacon, and Parmesan in a salad bowl. Drizzle with the dressing, and serve.

The Cobb Salad was invented at the Hollywood Brown Derby restaurant in 1928. It was named after the owner, Robert Cobb. There are many variations, but a true Cobb Salad always has chicken, lettuce, hard-boiled eggs, bacon, avocado, tomatoes, and is tossed with a red wine vinegar and Roquefort vinaigrette.

COBB salad

Vinaigrette

1/2	cup (120 ml) extra-virgin olive oil
1/4	cup (60 ml) red wine vinegar
1	tablespoon freshly squeezed lemon juice
1	teaspoon Dijon mustard
1/2	teaspoon Worcestershire sauce
1/2	teaspoon sugar
1	clove garlic, minced
	Freshly ground sea salt and black pepper

Salad

5	ounces (150 g) sliced bacon, rinds removed
2	boneless skinless chicken breasts, cut into small cubes
1	head iceberg lettuce, shredded
1	head romaine lettuce, chopped
5	ounces (150 g) blue cheese, preferably Roquefort, crumbled
3	hard-boiled eggs, peeled and quartered lengthwise
4	medium vine tomatoes, coarsely chopped
1	avocado, peeled, pitted, and cut into cubes

Serves 6 • Preparation 15 minutes • Cooking 12–13 minutes
Difficulty 1

Vinaigrette

1. Combine the oil, vinegar, lemon juice, mustard, Worcestershire sauce, sugar, and garlic in a blender. Whizz until smooth. Season with salt and pepper. Whizz again briefly and set aside until ready to serve.

Salad

1. Heat a large frying pan over medium heat. Dry-fry the bacon until crisp and brown, about 5 minutes. Set aside on paper towels to drain and cool.

2. Cook the chicken in the bacon fat left in the pan until browned and cooked through, 7–8 minutes. Set aside with the bacon to cool.

3. Combine the two types of lettuce in a salad bowl. Add the blue cheese, bacon, eggs, tomatoes, chicken, and avocado. Drizzle with the dressing, toss gently, and serve.

If you liked this recipe, you will love these as well.

BLUE CHEESE & STRAWBERRY salad

GREEK salad

CHICKEN CAESAR salad

MOROCCAN salad

Salad

4   medium tomatoes
2   Lebanese or ordinary cucumbers
2   green bell peppers (capsicums)
1   small red onion

Dressing

5   tablespoons (75 ml) extra-virgin olive oil
1¹/₂   tablespoons red wine vinegar
1   clove garlic, minced
        Freshly ground sea salt and black pepper

Serves 4 • Preparation 15 minutes • Difficulty 1

Salad

1. Bring a saucepan of water to a boil over high heat. Score a cross in the base of the tomatoes. Blanch in the boiling water for 20 seconds then plunge into a bowl of iced water. Peel the tomatoes, cut in half crosswise, and squeeze gently to remove the seeds.

2. Cut the cucumbers in half lengthwise and remove and discard the seeds.

3. Finely dice the tomato, cucumber, bell pepper, and onion and place in a salad bowl.

Dressing

1. Whisk the oil, vinegar, and garlic in a small bowl. Season with salt and pepper.

2. Drizzle the dressing over the salad, toss, and serve.

FATTOUSH
(Lebanese pita bread salad)

Serves 4 • Preparation 15 minutes • Cooking 5–10 minutes • Difficulty 1

Salad

2	day-old pita breads
1/4	cup (60 ml) extra-virgin olive oil
1 1/2	teaspoons sumac + extra, to sprinkle
12	cherry tomatoes, halved
1	Lebanese cucumber, peeled, halved lengthwise, and sliced
2	radishes, thinly sliced into rounds
1/2	small red onion, thinly sliced
1/2	cup chopped fresh parsley
2	tablespoons chopped fresh mint
2	scallions (spring onions), thinly sliced
2	baby cos lettuces, torn

Dressing

1/4	cup (60 ml) extra-virgin olive oil
2	tablespoons freshly squeezed lemon juice
1	clove garlic, minced
	Freshly ground sea salt and black pepper

Salad

1. Preheat the oven to 350°F (180°C/gas 4). Tear the bread into 2 inch (5 cm) pieces. Place on a baking sheet, drizzle with the oil, and sprinkle with the sumac. Toss to coat.

2. Bake for 5–10 minutes, until crisp and golden brown.

3. Combine the tomatoes, cucumber, radishes, onion, parsley, mint, scallions, lettuce, and bread in a salad bowl. Toss well.

Dressing

1. Whisk the oil, lemon juice, and garlic in a small bowl. Season with salt and pepper.

2. Drizzle the dressing over the salad and toss to combine. Sprinkle with a little extra sumac, and serve.

Gado gado, also known as Lotek, is a traditional Indonesian dish. There are many variations, but they all consist of varying amounts of fresh or cooked vegetables served with a delicious peanut sauce. This is our favorite recipe.

GADO GADO
(Indonesian salad)

Salad

2	large potatoes, sliced
8	ounces (250 g) green beans, trimmed
5	cups (250 g) shredded cabbage
1	crisp lettuce
3	cups (150 g) fresh bean sprouts
15	cherry tomatoes, halved
3	hard-boiled eggs, halved lengthwise
1	onion, sliced
2	scallions (spring onions), chopped
2	fresh red chilies, seeded and finely chopped
2	tablespoons finely chopped fresh parsley
1	tablespoon peanut oil
2	large eggs, beaten
$1/4$	teaspoon sea salt flakes
1	cup (100 g) fresh pineapple chunks

Sauce

1	tablespoon soy sauce
1	tablespoon lemon juice
6	tablespoons crunchy peanut butter
1	teaspoon red pepper flakes
$1/2$	teaspoon sea salt flakes
2	teaspoons sugar
$3/4$	cup (180 ml) coconut milk
2	tablespoons peanut oil

Serves 6 • Preparation 20 minutes + 15 minutes to cool • Cooking 15–20 minutes • Difficulty 2

Salad

1. Put the potatoes in a steamer and steam until almost tender, about 5 minutes. Add the green beans and cabbage and steam until tender but still crisp, 4–5 minutes. Set aside to cool for 15 minutes.

2. Use the lettuce leaves to line a large salad bowl. Arrange the cooled potato, green beans, cabbage, and bean sprouts on top. Cover with alternate pieces of tomato and hard-boiled egg and arrange the onion, scallions, and chilies on top. Sprinkle with the parsley.

3. Heat the oil in a medium frying pan over medium heat and pour in the beaten eggs, spreading thinly over the bottom. Season with salt. Cook until firm, then remove and set aside to cool.

4. Roll the omelet loosely and slice thinly. Place in the center of the salad. Add the pineapple chunks, and gently toss all the ingredients together.

Sauce

1. Place all the sauce ingredients in a small, heavy-bottomed saucepan over medium-low heat and bring to a boil, stirring constantly. Set aside to cool.

2. Pour the sauce over the salad, and serve.

WALDORF salad

Serves 2 • Preparation 10 minutes • Difficulty 1

Salad

2	organic, red-skinned apples, such as Cox's or Braeburn	1	cup (120 g) walnuts	
	Freshly squeezed juice of 1/2 lemon	2	cups (100 g) watercress	
3	stalks celery, cut into chunks			

Dressing

1/2	cup (120 ml) mayonnaise
1	tablespoon Dijon mustard

Salad

1. Cut the apples into chunks and toss with the lemon juice in a large salad bowl. Add the celery, walnuts, and watercress and toss gently.
2. Divide the salad between two serving bowls.

Dressing

1. Whisk the mayonnaise and mustard in a small bowl. Drizzle the dressing over the salads and serve.

GREEK ORZO salad

Serves 4 • Preparation 15 minutes • Cooking 5–10 minutes Difficulty 1

Salad

12	ounces (350 g) orzo (risone)	2	tablespoons capers
1	tablespoon extra-virgin olive oil	3	tablespoons pine nuts
5	ounces (150 g) feta cheese, crumbled		
1	red bell pepper (capsicum), chopped		
1	cup (100 g) olives, chopped		
4	scallions (spring onions), sliced		

Dressing

1/3	cup (90 ml) extra-virgin olive oil
1/3	cup (90 ml) fresh lemon juice
4	cloves garlic, minced
1	teaspoon Dijon mustard
1	teaspoon ground cumin
	Freshly ground sea salt and black pepper

Salad

1. Cook the orzo in a large pot of boiling salted water until al dente. Drain and cool in the colander for 5 minutes. Transfer to a bowl. Add the oil, feta, bell peppers, olives, scallions, and capers and toss well.

Dressing

1. Whisk all the ingredients in a small bowl.
2. Drizzle on the salad. Top with the pine nuts and serve.

CALABRIAN salad

Serves 4–6 • Preparation 15 minutes + 30 minutes to soak Cooking 20 minutes • Difficulty 2

Salad

3	red onions, peeled and sliced thinly
6	potatoes, unpeeled
8	plum tomatoes, sliced
15	fresh basil leaves, torn
1	tablespoon fresh oregano sprigs

Dressing

1/2	cup (120 ml) extra-virgin olive oil
3	tablespoons white or red wine vinegar
	Freshly ground sea salt and black pepper

Salad

1. Put the onions in a bowl of cold water and let soak for 30 minutes. Drain well.
2. Cook the potatoes in salted boiling water until tender, about 20 minutes. Drain and set aside until just cool enough to handle. Slip off the skins and slice thinly.
3. Arrange slices of potatoes, tomatoes, and onions on four serving plates. Top with basil and oregano.

Dressing

1. Whisk the oil, vinegar, salt, and pepper in a small bowl.
2. Drizzle over the salads, and serve.

PINZIMONIO

Serves 4 • Preparation 15 minutes • Difficulty 1

4–6	fresh artichokes	1/2	cup (120 ml) extra-virgin olive oil
	Lemon wedges		White wine vinegar
12	baby carrots	1/3	cup (90 ml) freshly squeezed lemon juice
2	small fennel bulbs		Freshly ground sea salt and black pepper
1	celery heart		
12	radishes		
6	scallions (spring onions)		

1. Trim the artichokes and slice the hearts thinly lengthwise. Rub with the lemon wedges to stop them from turning brown.
2. Scrub the carrots, leaving whole with the tops.
3. Discard the outermost layer of the fennel leaves and slice the bulbs thinly from top to bottom.
4. Cut the celery heart lengthwise in half or quarters.
5. Trim and wash the radishes.
6. Trim the scallions, leaving the green tops attached.
7. Arrange all the vegetables on a large serving platter. Fill small bowls with oil, vinegar, lemon juice, salt, and pepper and let each diner dip their vegetables.

INDEX